Attaining the 2030 Sustainable Development Goal of No Poverty

FAMILY BUSINESSES ON A MISSION

Griffith UNIVERSITY
Queensland, Australia

Series Editor:

Naomi Birdthistle

The Family Businesses on a Mission series examines how the United Nations Sustainable Development Goals (UN SDGs) can be applied in family businesses around the world, providing insights into cultural and societal differences and displaying innovative approaches to complex environmental and societal issues.

Other Titles in This Series

Attaining the 2030 Sustainable Development Goal of No Poverty

EDITED BY

NAOMI BIRDTHISTLE
Griffith University, Australia

emerald
PUBLISHING

United Kingdom – North America – Japan – India – Malaysia – China

Emerald Publishing Limited
Emerald Publishing, Floor 5, Northspring, 21-23 Wellington Street, Leeds LS1 4DL

First edition 2025

Reprints and permissions service
Contact: www.copyright.com

British Library Cataloguing in Publication Data
A catalogue record for this book is available from the British Library

ISBN: 978-1-83608-573-7 (Print)
ISBN: 978-1-83608-570-6 (Online)
ISBN: 978-1-83608-572-0 (Epub)

INVESTOR IN PEOPLE

Contents

List of Figures and Tables

About the Editor

Professor Naomi Birdthistle has entrepreneurship and family business running through her veins. She tried to work in her family business when she was four but was told she was too small. She came back year after year asking to work, and eventually her grandmother capitulated and left her work in the family business when she was seven. After years of working in the family business part-time and having completed her studies at Stirling University, Babson College, Harvard University, and the University of Limerick, Naomi established her own consulting business, consulting family businesses in her hometown. She is now a Professor of Entrepreneurship and Business Innovation at Griffith University, teaching future family business leaders and researching family business issues as well. Naomi is an award-winning academic having received numerous awards for her teaching and her research.

About the Contributors

Bettina Lynda Bastian is a Full Professor in Management at the American University in Bulgaria. Her research focuses on the intersections of gender, culture, governance, policy and organisation associated with entrepreneurship and innovation. Her research is internationally recognised for translating social science into work policies and practices that promote entrepreneurship and sustainable business, especially women's professional development and capacity building. She has been working in diverse senior university roles such as Dean of the College of Business and Law at the Royal University for Women in Bahrain and Head of Academic Programs in Entrepreneurship and Innovation at the Holy Spirit University of Kaslik, Lebanon (USEK). Prof Bastian also serves as Joint Editor in Chief for Gender, Work and Organization (GWO).

Allan Discua Cruz is the Director of the Centre for Family Business and a member of the Pentland Centre for Sustainability in Business and at Lancaster University Management School (United Kingdom). His current research interests relate to entrepreneurship by families in business. He has published in journals such as *Entrepreneurship and Regional Development, Journal of Business Research, Journal of Business Ethics, Entrepreneurship Theory and Practice, International Journal of Entrepreneurial Behaviour and Research, Journal of Family Business Management* and *International Small Business Journal,* among others. He is currently co-editing a special issue on entrepreneurship and poverty in the *Entrepreneurship and Regional Development Journal.* He has published three cases in this series related to SDG#8, SDG#11 and SDG#13.

Jacinta Dsilva is a Research Director at SEE Institute, a hub for sustainability research, education and innovation in Dubai, United Arab Emirates. In her current role, she spearheads the research department and focuses on areas such as sustainability, behavioural studies and circular economy in the built environment sector. She completed her PhD from Coventry University, UK, and holds two Master's degrees in Consumer Behaviour and Human Resources Management. She is the author of several books such as 'Business Communication' and 'Surviving the COVID-19 Pandemic' and 'SDG-5: Gender Equality & Female Empowerment Policy for Sustainable Development'. She has several research publications under her belt both in marketing and sustainability. Another area of interest is researching on family-run businesses that have developed a sustainable model of operations that has positively impacted the society at large. These research studies highlight that businesses successfully balance growth and social responsibility, serving as models for sustainable entrepreneurship.

Antoinette Flynn is an Associate Professor of Accounting and Finance at the Kemmy Business School, University of Limerick. With over two decades of experience, she specialises in financial accounting, entrepreneurial finance, and women and minority entrepreneurship. Her prolific research portfolio includes national and international collaborations, focusing on advancing the United Nations Sustainable Development Goals (SDGs). Dr Flynn's work on executive compensation and sustainable business practices intersects with corporate sustainability (SDG#12) and economic growth (SDG#8). Her research on gender equality in the accounting profession contributes to SDG#5, while her studies on carbon performance and financial performance explore the relationship between environmental sustainability (SDG#13) and financial outcomes. Dr Flynn has received multiple teaching awards and nominations, reflecting her innovative pedagogical approaches. She has also held academic leadership roles, including Assistant Dean, Academic Affairs, demonstrating her expertise in curriculum development and academic governance.

Brian Gregory is the Director of the Lancaster Entrepreneurs in Residence Programme, a member of the Pentland Centre for Sustainability in Business and the Centre for Family Business at the Lancaster University Management School (United Kingdom). His research interest lies in entrepreneurship, entrepreneurial fear, networks and the recognition and management of emotions within entrepreneurship. As a practitioner, he has created and divested businesses previously and holds several non-executive roles with organisations around the United Kingdom; he blends this wealth of experience with his work at Lancaster University.

Rob Hales is the Discipline Leader for Sustainable Business and Management in the Department of Business Strategy and Innovation. His research interests focus on the governance issues around the grand challenges of our time. Furthermore, his research focuses on SDGs in business and government, a business case for climate change, climate change policy, carbon management, sustainable tourism and working with First Peoples on consent processes and climate change. He was the first programme director of Griffith University's Master of Global Development. He teaches in the Department of Business Strategy and Innovation and has convened Master's level courses such as Leadership for Sustainable Business, Research Methods for Policy Makers and Sustainability and Systems Thinking. He supervises PhD students in the areas of collaborative governance, sustainability transitions and climate change.

Aditi Mishra is an Assistant Professor at Symbiosis School of Economics, Pune. With a PhD in Economics, she has been in academia since 2013. She has a strong research background in the intersection of E-governance, Gender and Education. She has presented research papers in several national and international conferences and has published in prestigious journals.

Sylvia B. Mwansa is the Founder and CEO of SBM Investments Limited, specialising in fashion, training and consulting. A passionate speaker on mindset change and personal motivation, she authored 'Mindset Change is Possible' and developed the 'My Process to Mindset Change® Program'. Known for her organisational skills and communication abilities, she serves as an Entrepreneur in Residence at Lancaster University, UK, and an Executive Consul member for the Great Lakes Region Private Sector Forum. Dr Mwansa contributes to society through charity work with Ladies Circle International and Agora Club Zambia, mentoring young entrepreneurs and supporting women and youth. Her research on foreign exchange fluctuations and SME growth in Zambia reflects her problem-solving drive. She advocates for Sickle Cell Disease and Childhood Cancer awareness and founded the Sustainable Business Mentorship Foundation to support start-ups, retirement and career changes.

Poh Yen Ng is an Associate Professor of Entrepreneurship and Innovation at Aberdeen Business School, Robert Gordon University. She holds a PhD in Management from the University of Canterbury, New Zealand, and is currently a Senior Fellow of Advance HE in the United Kingdom. Poh Yen grew up in a family business and ran an education franchise with her husband in Malaysia in the 2000s. She then ventured into academia to pass on her business experiences to university students. This later motivated her to develop a research passion for entrepreneurship, particularly the family business. Her research outputs cover many areas within the entrepreneurship and family business discipline, including the influence of socioemotional wealth in the family business, the empowerment process and social network dynamics of women entrepreneurs and the environmental practices of small and medium-sized enterprises.

Niharika Singh is an Assistant Professor at Symbiosis School of Economics, Pune. With a doctorate in Labour Economics, she has been in academia since 2009. She has taught at colleges in Jaipur and Bangalore earlier. Her major work areas are labour, gender and development economics. She has presented research papers at several national and international conferences and has publications in some reputed journals.

Bronwyn Wood is an Associate Professor of Marketing at the College of Business and Economics, United Arab Emirates (UAE) University, the national university of the UAE. She received her degrees all in Marketing from the Universities of Otago and Victoria (Wellington) in her native New Zealand. Coming to academia full-time in 2013, she has worked across the Gulf, in Saudi Arabia, Oman and now, the UAE. In addition, she has held academic posts in New Zealand and lived in Japan for several years. Dr Wood is on the editorial boards of all the leading Islamic marketing journals and is a Joint Editor in Chief for Gender, Work and Organization. She has published in tourism, Islamic marketing, cultural methodologies (Māori and Islamic), education and (women's) entrepreneurship. Outside her academic work, she runs a Muslim Market business consultancy, www.MuslimMarketingMatters.com, which focuses on doing business with Muslim consumers/markets wherever they are in the world.

Foreword

Prof. Walter Leal Filho (PhD, DSc, DPhil, DTech, DEd)
Chair, Inter-University Sustainable Development Research Programme

The Sustainable Development Goals (SDGs) adopted by the United Nations General Assembly in September 2015 provide a universal call to action to end poverty, protect the planet and ensure that by 2030 all people enjoy peace and prosperity.

They also entail elements of importance towards a strategic business engagement with sustainability issues. These offer a framework which provides businesses with a systematic approach to identify new business opportunities while contributing to the solution of the grand sustainability challenges facing the world today, including climate change. Each SDG, if achieved, will have a direct and significant positive impact on millions of people's lives around the world and the environment in which they live. Businesses have an opportunity to widen the purpose of business through adopting the SDGs as targets for their operations. Thus, they can make a meaningful contribution to the greater good through achieving their operational objectives.

Family businesses are uniquely placed to contribute to SDGs for many reasons. Firstly, because family business models have longer time perspectives, and this allows the family business to link with the longer term SDG time frame – 2030. Second, family businesses often focus on aspects of business operation which do not have an immediate return on investment such as relationship building with stakeholder groups. Thirdly, family businesses tend to rate the importance of ethics higher than standard businesses and thus align well with the social dimensions of the SDGs. Lastly, family businesses have intergenerational perspectives which is a core principle of sustainability.

This book provides insights into how family business operationalises SDG#1: No Poverty. The book uses a rigorous case study approach for family businesses to detail aspects of their business which help to overcome poverty. The cases provided here are living proof that family businesses that operate for the greater good actually work! Non-family businesses can take a leaf out of the family businesses portrayed in this book as they can provide different perspectives on how businesses can successfully align SDGs and business strategy.

Despite many businesses having adopted environmental social governance strategies and environmental management systems, the effect of this activity has not been reflected in a healthier planet. Many 'state of the environment' reports indicate that planetary health is decreasing, and planetary boundaries are being crossed or are about to be crossed. While the cause of this decline is not entirely the fault of business, there still needs to be a greater effort to address the decline. The challenge for family businesses is to use their unique characteristics and set ambitious programmes of work that make a meaningful contribution to achieving global goals. This book provides insights into how family businesses can achieve such a mission and how non-family businesses can be inspired to do the same.

Acknowledgements

The Editor would like to thank the contributors of the book for providing insights and sharing learnings from their business practice. We acknowledge that writing up cases in the format required considerable time and effort. The quality of the cases presented is testament to their efforts.

The Editor would also like to thank Emerald Publishing for supporting the publication of this book and the mission for deeper sustainability through utilising the SDGs.

Associate Professor Antoinette Flynn, author of Chapter 3, wishes to sincerely thank Tom Watson and Geraldine O'Connor for their valued contribution and input to this chapter.

Dr Mishra and Dr Singh, authors of Chapter 6, have stated that their chapter would not have been possible without the contributions of the staff at 'Naani's Litti Chokha'. They extend their sincere appreciation to Mr Abhishek Kumar, the business owner, for his invaluable support and willingness to provide the detailed information necessary to refine this chapter.

Dr Jacinta Dsilva, the author of Chapter 7, would like to take this opportunity to express her heartfelt gratitude to Ayesha Khan for generously sharing her valuable time for the interview and giving her valuable information to complete this case. Dr Dsilva would also like to sincerely thank Lydia Cherian for her unwavering support as a research assistant, which greatly contributed to the success of this case. Thank you both for your invaluable contributions.

Chapter 1

The Sustainable Development Goals: SDG#1 and Family Business

Rob Hales

Griffith University, Australia

Introduction

The 2030 Agenda for Sustainable Development, adopted by all member states of the United Nations in 2015, is a shared blueprint for people and the planet, intending to achieve peace and prosperity for all. The Sustainable Development Goals (SDGs) is a call to action to develop innovative solutions to some of the world's most complex, societal and environmental challenges. Businesses play a crucial role in forging this path. Family businesses account for more than two-thirds of businesses worldwide and contribute to 70–90% of the world's gross domestic product (GDP), and because of this, we believe it is important to showcase the role they play in facilitating the achievement of these SDGs. The 2030 Agenda for Sustainable Development is a call to action for all countries to address the global challenges of poverty, inequality, climate change, environmental degradation, peace and justice. These challenges are identified by 17 SDGs as depicted in Fig. 1.1 and within the SDGs are a total of 169 targets.

The 17 SDGs acknowledge that ending poverty and other global challenges need strategies that improve health and education, reduce inequality and spur economic growth – all while tackling climate change and working to preserve our oceans and forests (United Nations, 2021). When using the SDG goals as a strategy to improve the elements within any goal it is vital to use specific targets of each goal. These targets then need to be translated into business action. The main targets within SDG#1 *End poverty in all its forms everywhere* are shown in Table 1.1.

How Family Businesses Make Contributions to the SDG#1 Target

This book makes an important contribution to research on family businesses by highlighting how businesses can make valuable contributions towards these targets.

Attaining the 2030 Sustainable Development Goal of No Poverty, 1–12
Copyright © 2025 Rob Hales
Published under exclusive licence by Emerald Publishing Limited
doi:10.1108/978-1-83608-570-620241001

SUSTAINABLE DEVELOPMENT GOALS

1 NO POVERTY	2 ZERO HUNGER	3 GOOD HEALTH AND WELL-BEING	4 QUALITY EDUCATION	5 GENDER EQUALITY	6 CLEAN WATER AND SANITATION
7 AFFORDABLE AND CLEAN ENERGY	8 DECENT WORK AND ECONOMIC GROWTH	9 INDUSTRY, INNOVATION AND INFRASTRUCTURE	10 REDUCED INEQUALITIES	11 SUSTAINABLE CITIES AND COMMUNITIES	12 RESPONSIBLE CONSUMPTION AND PRODUCTION
13 CLIMATE ACTION	14 LIFE BELOW WATER	15 LIFE ON LAND	16 PEACE, JUSTICE AND STRONG INSTITUTIONS	17 PARTNERSHIPS FOR THE GOALS	SUSTAINABLE DEVELOPMENT GOALS

Fig. 1.1.   17 Sustainable Development Goals. *Source:* United Nations (2021). https://www.un.org/sustainabledevelopment/ *Notes:* The content of this publication has not been approved by the United Nations and does not reflect the views of the United Nations or its officials or Member States.

Table 1.1. SDG#1 Targets.

SDG#1 Targets	SDG#1 Indicators
1.1 By 2030, eradicate extreme poverty for all people everywhere, currently measured as people living on less than $1.25 a day	1.1.1 Proportion of the population living below the international poverty line by sex, age, employment status and geographic location (urban/rural)
1.2 By 2030, reduce at least by half the proportion of men, women and children of all ages living in poverty in all its dimensions according to national definitions	1.2.1 Proportion of population living below the national poverty line, by sex and age
1.2.2 Proportion of men, women and children of all ages living in poverty in all its dimensions according to national definitions
1.3 Implement nationally appropriate social protection systems and measures for all, including floors, and by 2030, achieve substantial coverage of the poor and the vulnerable	1.3.1 Proportion of population covered by social protection floors/systems, by sex, distinguishing children, unemployed persons, older persons, persons with disabilities, pregnant women,

Table 1.1. *(Continued)*

SDG#1 Targets	SDG#1 Indicators
	newborns, work-injury victims and the poor and the vulnerable
1.4 By 2030, ensure that all men and women, in particular the poor and the vulnerable, have equal rights to economic resources as well as access to basic services, ownership and control over land and other forms of property, inheritance, natural resources, appropriate new technology and financial services, including microfinance	1.4.1 Proportion of population living in households with access to basic services 1.4.2 Proportion of total adult population with secure tenure rights to land, (a) with legally recognised documentation, and (b) who perceive their rights to land as secure, by sex and by type of tenure
1.5 By 2030, build the resilience of the poor and those in vulnerable situations and reduce their exposure and vulnerability to climate-related extreme events and other economic, social and environmental shocks and disasters	1.5.1 Number of deaths, missing persons and directly affected persons attributed to disasters per 100,000 population 1.5.2 Direct economic loss attributed to disasters in relation to global gross domestic product (GDP) 1.5.3 Number of countries that adopt and implement national disaster risk reduction strategies in line with the Sendai framework for Disaster risk reduction 2015–2030 1.5.4 Proportion of local governments that adopt and implement local disaster risk reduction strategies in line with national disaster risk reduction strategies
1.a Ensure significant mobilisation of resources from a variety of sources, including through enhanced development cooperation, in order to provide adequate and predictable means for developing countries, in particular least developed countries, to implement programmes and policies to end poverty in all its dimensions	1.a.1 Total official development assistance grants from all donors that focus on poverty reduction as a share of the recipient country's gross national income 1.a.2 Proportion of total government spending on essential services (education, health and social protection)

(Continued)

Table 1.1. *(Continued)*

SDG#1 Targets	SDG#1 Indicators
1.b Create sound policy frameworks at the national, regional and international levels, based on pro-poor and gender-sensitive development strategies, to support accelerated investment in poverty eradication actions	1.b.1 Pro-poor public social spending

Source: United Nations (n.d.).

Family businesses can make a significant contribution to SDG#1 through specific actions that align with SDG#1 targets. Family businesses can use their influence and resources to advance the agenda of SDG#1, contributing not only to their organisational success but also to the broader societal goal of poverty eradication. Some of the ways family businesses can do this are as follows:

Target 1.1 Eradicating Extreme Poverty

Family firms can directly contribute to eradicating extreme poverty by implementing inclusive employment practices that provide decent work and fair wages. Their long-term orientation and social embeddedness make family businesses more likely to engage in socially responsible practices aimed at uplifting local communities from extreme poverty (Memili et al., 2018). Providing stable employment opportunities is a direct pathway out of extreme poverty for many. However, providing decent employment opportunities at scale remains a major challenge, especially in developing economies with high poverty rates and limited formal job markets. Family businesses may also struggle with capacity constraints and lack of resources to implement large-scale poverty alleviation initiatives. It is also difficult to overcome cultural and social biases and ensure inclusive hiring practices.

Target 1.2 Reducing Poverty in all Dimensions

The holistic and socially oriented nature of family businesses positions them well to tackle multidimensional poverty through initiatives addressing diverse deprivations like lack of education, healthcare, housing, etc. (Irava & Moores, 2010). Their community ties motivate family firms to adopt a comprehensive approach to poverty alleviation beyond just income poverty. Tackling multidimensional poverty requires a holistic understanding of the interlinked deprivations as well as coordinated efforts across multiple domains like education, health, housing etc. Mobilising resources and expertise for such comprehensive programs can strain family business capacities.

Target 1.3 Implementing Social Protection

Family businesses tend to have a stronger commitment to employee welfare stemming from their socioemotional wealth priorities (Cennamo et al., 2012). This increases their propensity to offer robust social protection schemes like healthcare benefits, insurance, childcare support and other social safety net measures for employees and communities. Offering robust social protection benefits can be costly and complex, especially for smaller family businesses with limited resources and capabilities. Designing and administering comprehensive schemes like healthcare, insurance, childcare etc. requires specialised expertise that may not be readily available.

Target 1.4 Equal Economic Rights

The ethical values and diversity goals of many family businesses drive them to promote equal economic rights and opportunities irrespective of gender or other status (Campopiano et al., 2017). They can provide equal access to resources like training, career growth, financial services and asset ownership for vulnerable groups. Deeply entrenched societal norms, discrimination and unequal power dynamics can hinder family firms' efforts to promote equal economic rights and opportunities. Overcoming unconscious biases and implementing truly inclusive policies requires deliberate effort and accountability. Access to resources like training, finance and assets is often restricted for vulnerable groups.

Target 1.5 Building Resilience

With their long-term sustainability mindset, family businesses are more inclined to implement eco-friendly practices that build resilience against economic disruption and climate impacts for the poor (Berrone et al., 2010). Their community ties also make them well-positioned partners for local resilience efforts like disaster preparedness and relief. Transitioning to eco-friendly and climate-resilient practices involves significant investments, technological upgradation and strategic reorientation which can be challenging for family businesses. Limited expertise, financial constraints and short-term pressures can disincentivise resilience-building measures.

Target 1.A Mobilising Resources

Family business' propensity for stakeholder engagement extends to partnerships that mobilise resources for poverty programs (Campopiano & De Massis, 2015). Their networks, political ties and commitment to social responsibility can facilitate collaborations channelling financing and technical resources for poverty eradication. Establishing productive cross-sector partnerships and mobilising resources like financing and technical know-how at a sufficient scale is a major obstacle. Family firms may lack experience in large-scale collaborations and face difficulties in attracting external partners and funders aligned with their poverty initiatives.

Target 1.B Pro-Poor Policy Frameworks

The societal embeddedness of family businesses often manifests in policy advocacy through industry associations and lobbying. This positions family businesses to constructively influence pro-poor and gender-sensitive policies enabling accelerated investment in poverty reduction strategies. Influencing policy making requires dedicated efforts in advocacy, lobbying and stakeholder engagement which can stretch family business capacities. Lack of unified voice and diverging priorities can dilute their policy impact (Tehubijuluw et al., 2021).

The research highlighted above identifies key issues relevant to each SDG target. There are several streams of research emerging in the literature on family business and sustainability that are relevant to this book. Ferreira et al. (2021) identify four streams of research in family business and sustainability: family business capital, family business strategy, family business social responsibility and family business succession. Family businesses that are aligned with the SDGs are more likely to have a positive impact on their financial performance (Rahim et al., 2022). Consumers and investors increasingly favour companies that demonstrate a commitment to sustainability. Lastly, many family businesses see themselves as ethical leaders and their commitment to ethical decision-making and responsible business conduct is enacted through business alignment and contribution to SDG#1.

The case study approach of this book provides insights into how SDG targets can be used to advance the family business's sustainability strategy and social responsibility concerning SDG#1. How a family's trans-generational sustainability intentions positively influence the strategy of the business and the family's concern for its reputation has been identified as a driver of sustainability in family businesses. Additionally, family businesses routinely combine innovation and tradition to achieve and maintain a sustainable competitive advantage.

Response Post-COVID-19 Pandemic

During the COVID-19 pandemic, many family businesses have shown to be more resilient and operate more sustainably than standard businesses (such as the shareholder approach). The reason for this lies in family businesses generally taking a long-term perspective on stakeholder relationships and the real need for long-term continuity planning to sustain the people within their businesses. The people in their business are most likely to be family members. However, like all businesses, the COVID-19 pandemic has placed financial pressures on family businesses. Based on these problems, we asked the question: How then can family businesses extend their capacity to operate more sustainably and with more social impact during times of business stress? We believe family businesses can offer unique insights into how sustainability and social impact can be part of the regenerative response to the impacts of the COVID-19 pandemic. This has implications for future business management and leadership in disruptive times.

The idea for the book came from two observations. The first observation was that family businesses that had sustainability at their core were performing well despite the impacts of the pandemic. The second observation was that the SDGs were being used as a framework for regeneration after the impact of the COVID-19 pandemic. The global pandemic of COVID-19 has presented challenges to those working towards achieving the goals. Effects of COVID-19 on the SDGs have had a negative effect. The social and economic impacts of COVID-19 have increased the divide between people living in rich and poor countries (Yuan et al., 2023). However, if there can be concerted action using the blueprint of the SDGs then human development can exceed pre-COVID-19 development trajectories (United Nations Environment Programme, 2021). What is needed is a combination of political commitment from all levels of government, investment in green economy initiatives, socially oriented innovation and a (re)focus on the purpose of business to align with the SDGs.

The importance of family businesses in their contribution to SDGs can be envisaged in several ways. First, many family business owners emphasise that the SDGs align with their core values and legacy-building efforts. They use the goals as a chance to align their business activities with a greater purpose and create a positive impact in their communities. Because of the nature of family businesses, they adopt a business purpose that provides a legacy for future generations. This results in a long-term perspective on business development and strategy. Family businesses also recognise that addressing the SDGs can enhance relationships with stakeholders, including customers, employees and local communities. Contributing to the achievement of the SDGs can foster goodwill and strengthen their reputation because of the external focus on global goals as opposed to just their own business goals (Barrett, 2017).

Challenges Facing Businesses in the Achievement of SDG#1

Family businesses are well-positioned to contribute to SDG#1 by promoting poverty eradication, but they face various challenges in their efforts. Overcoming these challenges will ensure a larger contribution to SDG#1. Many of the following challenges are noted by the family businesses showcased in this book. The first challenge is about resources. Resource constraints pose a significant challenge for many family businesses due to their relatively modest scale compared to larger corporations. These businesses often contend with limited financial means and a smaller workforce, which can hinder their capacity to invest comprehensively in initiatives centred on poverty alleviation. Striking a balance between these aspirations and other pressing demands becomes difficult, given the myriad competing priorities that family businesses must navigate. While pursuing profitability, growth and generational succession, achieving poverty eradication objectives necessitates careful planning to harmonise the priorities and multiple objectives.

Lack of expertise further compounds the challenge, as the implementation of effective poverty alleviation programs often requires specialised knowledge that might be beyond the reach of family businesses. Constraints on resources can hinder the hiring of experts or the development of in-house capabilities to adeptly design and manage such initiatives. Furthermore, resistance to change emerges as a notable hurdle, particularly for family businesses with long-term established operational traditions. Introducing new poverty-related policies, practices or cultural shifts may meet resistance from both employees and family members, impeding the integration of poverty eradication measures.

Family businesses, in contrast to larger corporations, often encounter limited access to networks that could otherwise assist with their sustainability activities. The broader collaborations and partnerships that large companies can establish might not be as readily accessible for family businesses, affecting their ability to achieve poverty eradication objectives. Despite their long-term perspective, these businesses also face the pressure to demonstrate short-term results. This leads to the reduced prioritisation of poverty alleviation initiatives that are not going to bring immediate financial returns. The distinctive dynamics inherent in family-owned enterprises, particularly concerning family members as employees and potential successors, can influence the implementation of poverty eradication initiatives.

Managing relationships, addressing expectations and mitigating potential conflicts among family members can impact the introduction of effective poverty alleviation measures. Additionally, regulations pose a formidable hurdle, especially in industries with stringent labour and social welfare regulations. Family businesses, often constrained by limited legal and compliance resources, are challenged by adhering to complex regulatory frameworks. Engaging with external stakeholders for poverty-related initiatives requires concerted effort, time and proficient communication. Despite their strong community ties, family businesses must devote considerable resources to effectively engage with their communities in endeavours to promote poverty eradication. Finally, the measurement of impact emerges as a challenging endeavour, one that family businesses might find particularly difficult due to limitations in tools and expertise. Despite these challenges, family businesses can overcome them by focusing on their strengths, values and commitment to long-term sustainability. Engaging in partnerships and aligning poverty eradication initiatives with core business values can help family businesses make meaningful contributions to SDG#1 while addressing the challenges they may encounter.

The Chapters and Contribution to SDG#1

Chapter 3 in this book is the case study on the Warm Age Wood Company which is a family-run social enterprise in County Durham, England. The way in which it contributes to SDG#1 is through combatting fuel poverty by combining the sale of sustainable wood briquettes with a community-driven knitting initiative. The Warm Age Wood Company's business model is intricately tied to achieving SDG#1 by providing free or subsidised heating fuel to those in need. They also engage a network of volunteer knitters who create woolen items for sale with proceeds funding the purchase of more briquettes for distribution. This approach fosters community engagement and provides meaningful activity for local older residents. The chapter showcases how a business model of a small family-run businesses can play significant role in addressing complex social issues like poverty while operating a viable business. The Warm Age Wood Company exemplifies how businesses can contribute meaningfully to SDG#1.

Chapter 4 provides that case of Simply Best Merchandise (SBM) Investments Limited which is a family-owned business in Zambia, founded in 1994. SBM's alignment with SDG#1 (No Poverty) is evident through targeted coaching, educational programs and mentoring to aspiring entrepreneurs The Mindset Change Process is central to their approach which targets cultural and behavioural barriers that perpetuate poverty. Additionally, SBM collaborates with government agencies, non-profit organisations and other stakeholders to create a comprehensive approach to poverty alleviation. SBM's business model not only generates revenue but also actively contributes to poverty reduction SDG#1 through these business activities.

Chapter 5 examines Fig Holding is a family-run enterprise in Lebanon. It makes a contribution to achieving SDG#1 (No Poverty) through its business practices and community engagement. Fig Holding operates in the culinary and hospitality industry, with its flagship brand Mayrig offering authentic Armenian cuisine. Fig Holding contributes to SDG#1 by providing employment and income stability to over 120 people in a volatile economic environment. Through its Kamakian brand, it supports local farmers, particularly women, sourcing products from over 400 Lebanese farmers. The business has also engaged in significant humanitarian efforts during crises, such as providing meals to thousands of people after the 2020 Beirut port explosion and supporting displaced Armenians from Nagorno-Karabakh. The business model emphasises local sourcing and supports small-scale producers which contributes to rural development and poverty reduction. Fig Holding's approach to business demonstrates that commercial success can be aligned with significant social responsibility and community engagement contributing to SDG#1.

Chapter 6 provides the case of Naani's Litti Chokha – a small family-owned restaurant in Pune, India. The case demonstrates how small businesses can significantly contribute to SDG#1 in the hospitality sector. The restaurant addresses multiple SDG#1 targets through its business practices and employment policies. Naani's Litti Chokha ensures employees receive over 110 Indian Rupees per day and this has led to substantial improvements in employees' financial situations, with examples of increased savings and loan repayments. The restaurant reduces poverty (SDG#1.2) by employing both men and women, improving family living standards and offering affordable, nutritious food to low-income individuals. Naani's Litti Chokha also implements micro-level social protection measures (SDG#1.3) by prioritising employee health, providing financial inclusion through bank account payments and supporting education for employees' children. The business promotes equal rights to economic resources (SDG#1.4) by enhancing employee skills, facilitating asset building through land ownership and enabling access to financial services. Despite challenges such as rising costs and seasonal fluctuations, Naani's Litti Chokha's approach demonstrates how small-scale, locally focused initiatives can effectively combat poverty while maintaining a profitable business.

The last chapter provides that case of 'Food ATM' from the United Arab Emirates. This is a social enterprise founded by Ayesha Khan and her husband Sajid Khan in 2019. The Food ATM project directly addresses SDG#1 by providing affordable, nutritious meals to blue-collar workers and low-income expatriates in the UAE. By offering meals for at a drastically reduced rate (around 3 AED), Food ATM helps alleviate financial burdens on workers which then allows them to direct more personal finance towards education, healthcare and supporting their families back home. The initiative also promotes sustainable practices by reducing food waste through partnerships with grocery stores and implementing a food exchange programme. The chapter highlights how empathy-driven social entrepreneurship can address poverty and food insecurity aligning with SDG#1.

The integration of sustainability into the business strategies family businesses can lead to the development of innovative products, services and business models that contribute to the greater good as well as create business value. Family business owners also use SDGs to identify and mitigate risks associated with environmental, social and governance issues. By addressing these challenges as a future-oriented strategy, they aim to ensure the resilience and long-term success of their businesses (Bauweraerts et al., 2022).

Conclusion

Family businesses have a pivotal role to play in achieving SDG#1. With their deep roots in local communities, long-term outlook and commitment to ethical practices, family firms are uniquely positioned to contribute to poverty eradication efforts through various avenues. By providing decent employment opportunities, investing in skill development programmes and adopting inclusive business models, family businesses can directly uplift individuals and communities from poverty. Their ability to integrate marginalised groups into value chains and offer affordable products and services tailored to the needs of the poor fosters economic empowerment and social inclusion.

The book series, which used a case-based approach, provides evidence of the role of family businesses in effectively contributing to all SDGs. The book is one of 17 vignette book series in which each book is comprised of a set of short, easy-to-read family business cases related to the unique SDG being discussed in the book. The format of the book series allows the works to be accessible to those working in the field beyond academia such as family business practitioners, family business owners, family business advisors, government and business policy-makers, members of NGOs, business associations and philanthropic centres, as well as to those who have a general interest in entrepreneurship and business.

References

Barrett, R. (2017). *The values-driven organization: Cultural health and employee well-being as a pathway to sustainable performance.* Taylor & Francis.

Bauweraerts, J., Arzubiaga, U., & Diaz-Moriana, V. (2022). Going greener, performing better? The case of private family firms. *Research in International Business and Finance, 63,* 101784. https://doi.org/10.1016/j.ribaf.2022.101784

Berrone, P., Cruz, C., Gomez-Mejia, L. R., & Larraza-Kintana, M. (2010). Socioemotional wealth and corporate responses to institutional pressures: Do family-controlled firms pollute less? *Administrative Science Quarterly, 55*(1), 82–113. https://doi.org/10.2189/asqu.2010.55.1.82

Campopiano, G., & De Massis, A. (2015). Corporate social responsibility reporting: A content analysis in family and non-family firms. *Journal of Business Ethics, 129*(3), 511–534. https://doi.org/10.1007/s10551-014-2174-z

Campopiano, G., De Massis, A., Rinaldi, F. R., & Sciascia, S. (2017). Women's involvement in family firms: Progress and challenges for advancing gender equality in management and entrepreneurship. *European Management Journal, 35*(2), 210–222. https://doi.org/10.1016/j.emj.2016.07.005

Cennamo, C., Berrone, P., Cruz, C., & Gomez-Mejia, L. R. (2012). Socioemotional wealth and proactive stakeholder engagement: Why family-controlled firms care more about their stakeholders. *Entrepreneurship Theory and Practice, 36*(6), 1153–1173. https://doi.org/10.1111/j.1540-6520.2012.00543.x

Ferreira, J. J., Fernandes, C. I., Schiavone, F., & Mahto, R. V. (2021). Sustainability in family business–A bibliometric study and a research agenda. *Technological Forecasting and Social Change, 173,* 121077. https://doi.org/10.1016/j.techfore.2021.121077

Irava, W. J., & Moores, K. (2010). Clarifying the strategic advantage of familiness: Unbundling its dimensions and highlighting its paradoxes. *Journal of Family Business Strategy, 1*(3), 161–165. https://doi.org/10.1016/j.jfbs.2010.08.002

Memili, E., Fang, H., Koc, B., Yildirim-Öktem, Ö., & Sonmez, S. (2018). Sustainability practices of family firms in the tourism and hospitality industry. *Cornell Hospitality Quarterly, 59*(1), 82–98.

Rahim, N. A. A. A., Muhmad, S. N., Abidin, A. F. Z., Muhmad, S. N., & Omar, K. (2022). A systematic review of corporate governance and sustainability performance: Pre-and post-sustainable development goals adoption period. *Management & Accounting Review, 21*(3), 1–36.

Shulla, K., Voigt, B. F., Cibian, S., Scandone, G., Martinez, E., Nelkovski, F., & Salehi, P. (2021). Effects of COVID-19 on the sustainable development goals (SDGs). *Discover Sustainability, 2,* 15.

Tehubijuluw, Z., Yusriadi, Y., Firman, H., & Rianti, M. (2021). Poverty alleviation through entrepreneurship. *Journal of Legal, Ethical and Regulatory Issues, 24*(1), 1.

United Nations. (2021). *The 17 goals.* United Nations. https://sdgs.un.org/goals

United Nations Environment Programme. (2021). *Leaving no one behind: Impact of COVID-19 on the sustainable development goals (SDGs).* United Nations Environment Programme. https://www.undp.org/publications/leaving-no-one-behind-impact-covid-19-sustainable-development-goals-sdgs

United Nations. (n.d.). *SDG indicators: Global indicator framework for the Sustainable Development Goals and targets of the 2030 Agenda for Sustainable Development.* United Nations. https://unstats.un.org/sdgs/indicators/indicators-list/

Yuan, H., Wang, X., Gao, L., Wang, T., Liu, B., Fang, D., & Gao, Y. (2023). Progress towards the sustainable development goals has been slowed by indirect effects of the COVID-19 pandemic. *Communications Earth & Environment, 4*(1), 184.

Zellweger, T. M., Nason, R. S., & Nordqvist, M. (2012). From longevity of firms to transgenerational entrepreneurship of families: Introducing family entrepreneurial orientation. *Family Business Review, 25*(2), 136–155. https://doi.org/10.1177/0894486511423531

Chapter 2

The Heart of Business: Understanding Family-Owned Ventures

Naomi Birdthistle

Griffith University, Australia

What Does It Mean to Be a Family Business?

The study of family businesses remains an emerging field within academia. However, a significant challenge persists due to the lack of a universally accepted definition for what constitutes a family business. Professor John Davis, a renowned expert in this area, has meticulously reviewed various definitions from existing literature and categorised them into two main types: structural definitions and process definitions (Davis, 2001). Structural definitions focus on ownership and management arrangements, such as the requirement that a family owns 51% or more of the business. In contrast, process definitions emphasise the family's level of engagement and influence in business operations and decision-making, reflecting their desire to maintain control over the company's direction. To highlight varying perspectives, Table 2.1 has been developed, which features definitions from influential researchers in the family business field. These definitions are categorised based on Davis's (2001) framework, distinguishing between structural and process viewpoints. This classification provides insight into the multifaceted approaches scholars and practitioners take when defining family businesses and understanding their core features.

In their research, Astrachan and Shanker (2003, p. 211) emphasise the absence of a concise, universally agreed-upon definition for family businesses, which complicates quantifying their overall impact. As a result, they devised a spectrum that allows for defining family businesses across a range – from broad to narrow (see Fig. 2.1).

This spectrum accounts for the diverse levels of family engagement within a business and provides varying degrees of specificity in the definition. Their proposed definitions include the following:

- Broad Definition: At the outer edge of the bull's eye, a family business involves some family participation, with the family controlling the strategic direction.

Attaining the 2030 Sustainable Development Goal of No Poverty, 13–25

Copyright © 2025 Naomi Birdthistle

Published under exclusive licence by Emerald Publishing Limited

doi:10.1108/978-1-83608-570-620241002

Table 2.1. Definitions of Family Businesses With a Structural or Process Lens Applied.

Family Business Definition	Author	Structural or Process Lens Applied
Members of one family own enough voting equity to control strategy, policy and tactical implementation	Miller and Rice (1967)	Process definition
Ownership control by a single family or individual	Barnes and Hershon (1976)	Structural definition
Two or more family members influence the direction of the business through the exercise of management roles, kinship ties or ownership rights	Davis and Tagiuri (1982)	Process definition
Family influence over business decisions	Dyer (1986)	Process definition
Ownership and operation by members of one or two families	Stern (1986)	Structural definition
Legal control over the business by family members	Lansberg et al. (1988)	Structural definition
Closely identified with at least two generations of a family, the link has had a mutual influence on the company policy and the interests and objectives of the family	Donnelley (1964)	Process definition
Expectation or actuality of succession by a family member	Churchill and Hatten (1987)	Process definition
Single-family effectively controls the firm through the ownership of greater than 50% of the voting shares and a significant portion of the firm's senior management team is drawn from the same family	Leach et al. (1990)	A mix of structural and process definitions

Even if only a few family members are involved, it qualifies as a family business.
• Middle Ground Definition: Moving towards the centre, this definition emphasises passing the business to a family member. Incumbent family members actively manage the business, preparing for the generational transition.

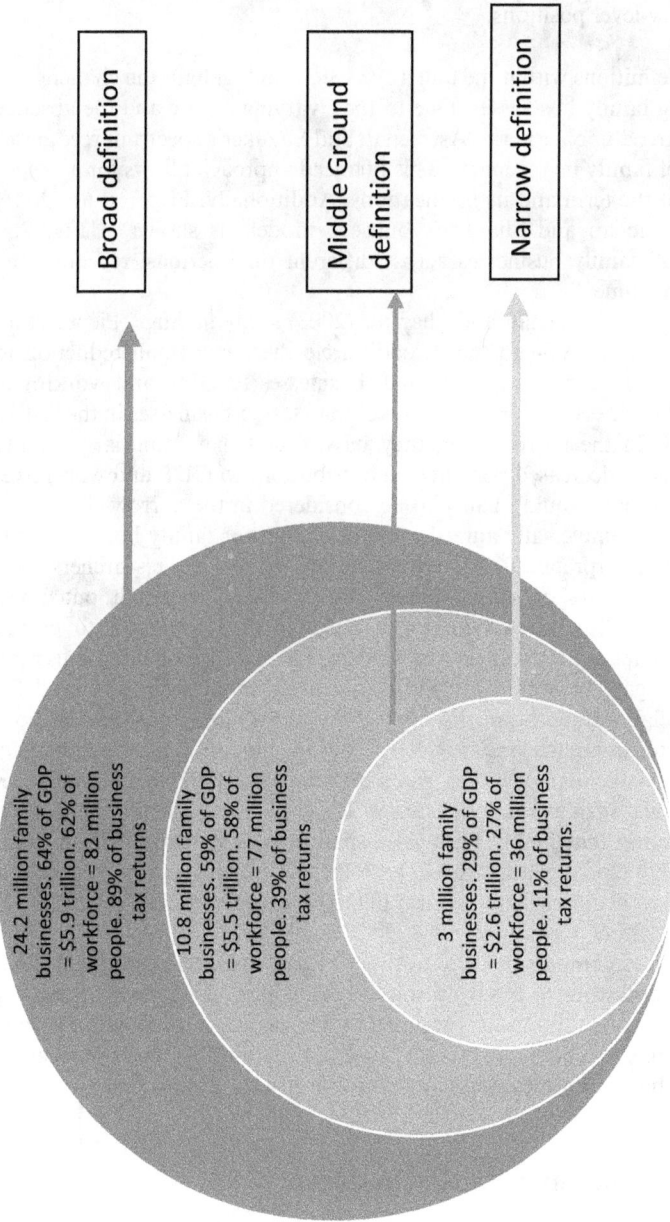

Broad definition

24.2 million family businesses. 64% of GDP = $5.9 trillion. 62% of workforce = 82 million people. 89% of business tax returns

Middle Ground definition

10.8 million family businesses. 59% of GDP = $5.5 trillion. 58% of workforce = 77 million people. 39% of business tax returns

Narrow definition

3 million family businesses. 29% of GDP = $2.6 trillion. 27% of workforce = 36 million people. 11% of business tax returns.

Fig. 2.1.   Defining Family Business: The Family Business Bull's-Eye. *Source:* Adapted from Astrachan and Shanker (2003, p. 218).

- Narrow Definition: At the core, extensive family involvement spans generations. Management includes family members from different age groups, including siblings and cousins in various roles and potentially younger relatives joining at entry-level positions.

The diverse definitions within the bull's eye spectrum highlight the challenge of precisely defining family businesses. Due to their varying nature and the absence of universally agreed-upon criteria, Astrachan and Shanker's spectrum recognises different levels of family involvement. This nuanced approach allows for a deeper understanding of the term and its implications. Additionally, Pieper et al. (2021) builds upon Astrachan and Shanker's bullseye model, as shown in Fig. 2.2, applying it to US family businesses across different time periods, revealing the growth in their volume.

In contrast to the Astrachan and Shanker (2003) study findings, Pieper et al. (2021) found that in relation to the 'Broad' circle there is a small reduction in results, i.e. decreased contribution of small businesses to GDP and workforce. Therefore, small businesses have grown slower than larger businesses in the last 18 years in the US. In the narrow ring, they have found that some large family businesses may have decreased percentage contributions to GDP and workforce. For example, Walmart would qualify to be considered in the narrow ring.

The absence of a universally agreed-upon definition for family businesses has resulted in diverse interpretations and criteria among writers and researchers. This lack of consensus raises concerns, potentially impacting research outcomes. Cano-Rubio et al. (2017) advocate for a single general criterion to ensure consistent and comparable results across studies. The absence of standardisation also highlights a gap in discussions within the field, emphasising the need for dialogue and collaboration. Some writers use the term 'family business' without clarity, leading to ambiguity and misinterpretation, hindering a comprehensive understanding. Confusion sometimes arises between family businesses and other types of enterprises, such as small businesses. It's crucial to differentiate between the two, considering that family businesses span a wide spectrum – from local small enterprises to global giants like LG and Bacardi. Notably, family businesses can be privately owned, but there are also publicly traded companies with family ownership (e.g. CBS & Viacom).

To address these complexities, the authors of the book selected respondents based on self-identification as family businesses. They then categorised them using structural or process definitions (as proposed by Davis (2001)), aiming for a more comprehensive understanding of family business dynamics. Their systematic approach contributes to a meaningful exploration of this vital sector.

Key Characteristics of a Family Business

Family businesses are not homogenous entities, and their characteristics can vary significantly based on various factors. The size, industry, culture and level of family involvement all contribute to the uniqueness of each family business. As a result,

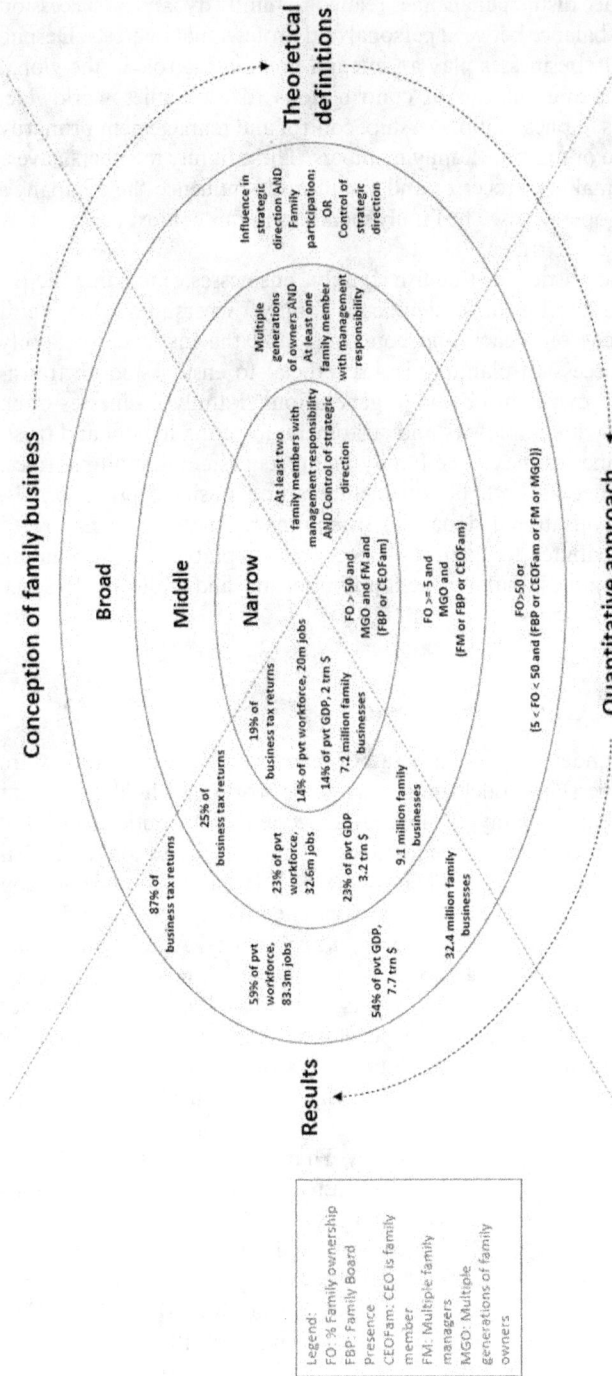

Fig. 2.2. Bullseye 2021. (Pieper et al., 2021, p. 15).

these businesses may face distinct challenges related to family dynamics, succession planning and finding a balance between personal and professional interests. Despite these differences, family businesses play an integral and diverse role in the global business landscape, making substantial contributions to economies worldwide. Being a family business implies that ownership, control and management primarily rest in the hands of one or multiple family members. These family members have a direct say in decision-making processes and significantly influence the company's strategic direction and operations. The family members in this context are typically those related by blood or marriage.

Several key characteristics distinguish family businesses, including active family involvement in the business, significant family ownership, a long-term orientation with a focus on legacy and continuity and the influence of family values and culture. Succession planning is also crucial to ensure smooth transitions of leadership and ownership between generations. Family businesses often prioritise relationships with employees and customers, fostering loyalty and trust. Moreover, family businesses may have family members assuming multiple roles, taking on responsibilities as both family members and business professionals, creating a unique organisational dynamic. In summary, the diverse nature of family businesses contributes to their resilience and adaptability in navigating challenges and opportunities, making them an important and enduring presence in the business world.

Family Businesses Around the World

Family businesses are undeniably a reality rather than an enigma. In fact, they are the most common ownership model found across the world and hold significant influence over the global economy. Their prevalence and contributions to GDP are immense and well-documented. The impact of family businesses on the global economy is not to be underestimated. Their longevity, adaptability and dedication to long-term sustainability are factors that have enabled them to thrive and make substantial contributions to economic growth and prosperity. As a result, family businesses are a vital and enduring aspect of the business landscape, and their presence and influence are felt across continents and industries. As per Tharawat Magazine (2023), Fig. 2.3 highlights the substantial contributions that family businesses make to global GDP. These data underscore their economic significance and the essential role they play in various industries and markets worldwide.

It is evident from the research produced by Tharawat Magazine (2023) that family businesses play a significant and important role in the economies of various nations and have cemented their impact on a nation's GDP, highlighting their enduring importance in the business landscape. In India, for example, family businesses contributed to a remarkable 79% of the country's GDP, and it is home to 15 of the world's largest 500 family businesses (Tharawat Magazine, 2023). This substantial contribution demonstrates the enduring strength and influence of family businesses in one of the world's largest economies. Similarly, in the United

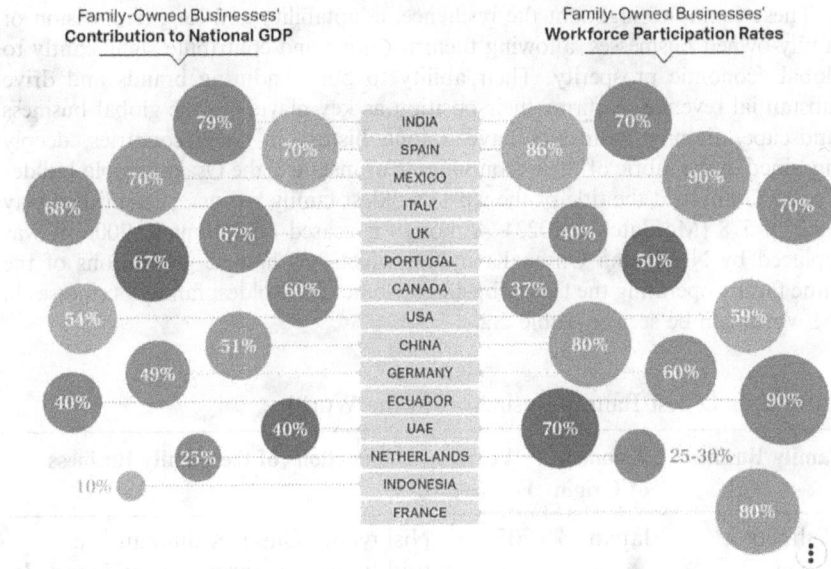

Fig. 2.3.   Global Assessment of Family-Owned Businesses: National
GDP Contribution and Workforce Participation. *Source:* Tharawat
Magazine (2023, para.5).

Arab Emirates, family businesses have a substantial presence, accounting for an
estimated 70% of employment. Their significant representation further illustrates
their role as a driving force in the UAE economy (Tharawat Magazine, 2023).

Family-owned businesses indeed play a pivotal role in the creation of global
wealth and are often significant contributors to revenue generation and economic
growth. The joint research conducted by the University of St. Gallen and Ernst
and Young reveals the substantial impact of family businesses on the global
economy. In 2023, the family businesses studied generated an astounding
$US8.02 trillion in revenue, representing a remarkable 10% increase from their
previous findings in 2021 (EY Global, 2023). The success of family-owned businesses is further exemplified by some of the world's most well-known and pros-
perous brands. Wal-Mart, owned by the Waltons, stands as a prime example,
with impressive revenues of $572.8 billion recorded in 2022. Additionally, the
company employed 2.3 million people worldwide in the same year, demonstrating
the scale of its operations and its impact on job creation (Walmart, 2023).
Likewise, the Porsche family's ownership of Volkswagen has played a crucial role
in the automotive giant's success. In 2021, Volkswagen's total revenues reached
US$18.8 billion, contributing significantly to the overall market revenue of
US$1.8 trillion for the same year (Statista Mobility Market Insights, 2022).

These examples highlight the resilience, adaptability and long-term vision of family-owned businesses, allowing them to thrive and contribute significantly to global economic prosperity. Their ability to build enduring brands and drive substantial revenue reaffirms their position as key players in the global business landscape. Family businesses have a long history in some countries, deeply ingrained in the fabric of their economies. For instance, the Osaka temple-builder Kongo Gumi held the title of the world's oldest family business, established way back in 578 (McClatchie, 2023). Although it ceased operations in 2006, it was replaced by Nishiyama Onsen Keiunkan which has had 52 generations of the same family operating the family business. Some of the oldest family businesses in the world can be seen in Table 2.2.

Table 2.2. Oldest Family Businesses in the World.

Family Business	Country of Origin	Year Founded	Functions of the Family Business
Nishiyama Onsen Keiunkan	Japan	705 AD	Nishiyama Onsen Keiunkan is a traditional hot spring inn in Japan. It holds the Guinness World Record for being the oldest hotel in continuous operation.
Hoshi Onsen Chojukan	Japan	718 AD	Hoshi Onsen Chojukan is a traditional Japanese hot spring inn located in the Ishikawa Prefecture. It is currently being led by the 46th generation of the Hoshi family.
Château de Goulaine	France	1000	Château de Goulaine is a castle and vineyard located in the Loire Valley France. It has been in the Goulaine family since it was established.
Barone Ricasoli	Italy	1141	Barone Ricasoli is one of the oldest wineries in Italy and is in Tuscany. It has remained under the ownership of the Ricasoli family for over 850 years
Richard de Bas	France	1326	Richard de Bas is a paper mill located in Ambert France. It has been operated by the Bas family for over 700 years and is known for producing high-quality handmade paper.
Antinori	Italy	1385	Antinori is another renowned winery in Tuscany Italy. It is one of the oldest family-run businesses specialising in wine production.

Table 2.2. *(Continued)*

Family Business	Country of Origin	Year Founded	Functions of the Family Business
Rentez-Vous	France	1394	Rentez-Vous is a French clothing business that has been passed down through generations of the Rentez family for more than 600 years.
Zildjian	Turkey/ USA	1623	Zildjian is renowned for manufacturing cymbals. The business was established in Turkey and later moved to the United States. It has remained family-owned for nearly 400 years.
Kikkoman	Japan	1630	Kikkoman is a well-known Japanese food company specialising in soy sauce and other condiments. It has been owned by the Mogi family for over 360 years.

Source: Authors own.

These examples underscore the enduring influence of family-owned businesses, significantly contributing to global economic activity and shaping commercial landscapes across diverse industries and regions. Research findings emphasise their ongoing impact on national economies, driven by adaptability, innovation and contributions to growth. As we peer into the future, family businesses remain pivotal in shaping economies and societies worldwide.

Countries Represented in This Book

The family businesses portrayed in this book come from England, Zambia, Lebanon, India and the UAE. In England, family businesses play a pivotal role in its economy. One of the oldest family businesses in England is R. J. Balson and Son Ltd, which is a butcher in Bridport, Dorest, which has been selling sausages and bacon since 1515, during the reign of Henry VIII (Agency, 2015). The Balson family's legacy continues to thrive, making them the oldest direct lineage family business in England. Other family businesses include JCB led by the Bamford family, which has a global footprint. Also, Burberry is a family business, which is known for its iconic trench coats, whose heritage dates to the 19th century. Warburtons, a household name in bread, remains family-owned and committed to quality.

Few studies have been conducted on family businesses in Zambia. Since Magasi (2016) found that most small and medium-sized enterprises (SMEs) are family run and SMEs play an important role in the Zambian economy we can assume that family businesses are active in Zambia. International Trade Centre (2020) report that SMEs represent 97% of all businesses, 70% of GDP and 88% of employment in Zambia therefore family businesses are active in the country. A family business that is interwoven into the fabric of the Zambian economy is Lusaka Laundry (Konge, 2014). This family business, which was established in the 1930s, by Pargji Ranchod with his wife Fulliben, is now run by Mr Rajen Rachod, who is the grandson of the founder.

In Lebanon, family businesses have a very active role in the economy. Zeidan (2021) reports that 1.05 million of the 1.24 million jobs are provided by family businesses and therefore represents 85% of the private sector. BerytechBeat (2019) found that family businesses account for more than 95% of all micro, small and medium-sized enterprises (MSMEs) in Lebanon, with only 5% being able to survive the transition from second to third generation. Family businesses in Lebanon have added challenges to running their business in the country, besides the 'typical' issues family businesses face such as succession, growth etc. Fares (2023, para. 1) reports that the economic and political situation in Lebanon has raised significant concerns about the future of family businesses. The country has been grappling with an ongoing economic crisis, compounded by the impact of the COVID-19 pandemic and the devastating Beirut port explosion in 2020. Despite these challenges, family businesses in Lebanon also have opportunities to adapt and innovate, ensuring their resilience and long-term viability. A family business that has stood the test of time in Lebanon is the Fattal Group, established in 1897, which is led by the great granddaughter of the founder, Caroline Fattal (Fattal, 2021). This family business employs 3,000 people, has 35,000 customers and can be found in multiple business sectors such as healthcare and office equipment (Forbes, 2024).

India has a rich history of multi-generational family businesses that have thrived over time, becoming integral to the country's economy. Mafatlal (2023) reports that family businesses constitute approximately 85% of all incorporated businesses in India. Furthermore, despite the rise of start-ups, family businesses still contribute significantly, accounting for 79% of India's annual GDP (Mafatlal, 2023). PwC's Family Business Survey (2023) shows how resilient and successful family businesses are in India by the very nature that 'an impressive 83% of enterprises experienced substantial growth while a mere 5% experienced reduction in sales' (PwC, 2023, para.4). Family businesses cross the full spectrum of MSMEs as well as large enterprises in India and have a long history in the Indian economy and includes names like: Tata Group – established in 1868, Reliance Industries – established 1929 and Bajaj Group – established in 1930 (SiliconIndia, 2014). One of the oldest family businesses in India is the Wadia Group, founded by Lovji Wadia who won the contract to manufacture ships and docks for the East India Company in 1736 (SiliconIndia, 2014). The family business today has expanded beyond building ships and ports, and now includes real estate, retail, healthcare, auto components and plantations for example in its business portfolio (The Wadia Group, 2010).

In the UAE, there are approximately 343,000 private sector businesses, including family businesses, which significantly contribute greatly to the national economy (Puri-Mirza, 2021). Abbas (2022) reports that in the UAE, family-owned businesses contributed to 70% of the UAE's GDP. The National (2023, para 6) is quoted as saying that up to '90 % of private companies in the country are family businesses, employing more than 70% of the sector's work-force.' According to Forbes Middle East, 21 UAE families were ranked among the Arab world's 100 most powerful family businesses – second highest in the region after Saudi Arabia (Varghese, 2021). At the highest level in the country, family businesses have also been identified as being important for the future of the UAE. Sheikh Mohammed bin Rashid, the Vice President, and Ruler of Dubai, is actively promoting the growth of family businesses in the UAE. He played a key role in setting up a new centre dedicated to scaling and supporting family enterprises. According to Cabral (2022), this programme aims to double the number of family businesses in the UAE, potentially boosting the GDP to $320 billion by 2032.

The Future of Family Businesses Post-COVID-19

During the COVID-19 pandemic, family businesses demonstrated a notable level of resilience compared to non-family businesses. Research conducted by Bajpai et al. (2021) on a global scale revealed that family businesses laid off fewer staff (8.5%) compared to non-family businesses (10.2%). This ability to retain more employees during challenging times highlights the resilience and adaptability of family businesses in the face of economic disruptions caused by the pandemic.

Due to their capacity to weather crises and make strategic decisions with a long-term perspective, Bajpai et al. (2021) argue that family businesses are posi-tioned to play a significant role in driving the global economic recovery from COVID-19. As the world continues to recover from the impacts of the pandemic, family businesses may emerge as key drivers of economic growth and stability, both at the local and global levels. The findings of this research suggest that family businesses' unique characteristics, such as strong family values, commit-ment to employees and focus on long-term sustainability, contributed to their ability to navigate the challenges brought about by the pandemic more effectively than other companies. As a result, they are expected to be instrumental in fostering economic recovery and rebuilding in the post-pandemic era.

References

Abbas, W. (2022, September 19). UAE: New initiative to turn 200 family businesses into major companies by 2023. *Khaleej Times*. https://www.khaleejtimes.com/business/uae-new-initiative-to-turn-200-family-businesses-into-major-companies-by-2030

Agency. (2015, September 22). Dorset butcher's that started as Henry VIII-era market stall is Britain's oldest family business. *The Telegraph*. https://www.telegraph.co.

uk/news/shopping-and-consumer-news/11882495/Dorset-butchers-that-started-as-Henry-VIII-era-market-stall-is-Britains-oldest-family-business.html

Astrachan, J. H., & Shanker, M. C. (2003, September). Family businesses' contribution to the U.S. economy: A closer look. *Family Business Review, 16*(3), 211–219.

Bajpai, A., Calabro, A., & McGinness, T. (2021). *Mastering a comeback: How family businesses are triumphing over COVID-19.* KPMG. https://assets.kpmg.com/content/dam/kpmg/ae/pdf-2021/02/Family-Business-Survey-Report.pdf

Barnes, L. B., & Hershon, S. A. (1976). Transferring power in the family business. *Harvard Business Review, 54*(4), 105–114.

BerytechBeat. (2019, August 9). Strengthening the governance of family businesses in Lebanon & the Mena region. *BerytechBeat.* https://berytech.org/strengthening-the-governance-of-family-businesses-in-lebanon-the-mena-region/

Cabral, A. (2022, September 19). New UAE initiative aims to double family businesses' contribution to GDP to $320 bn by 2032. *The National.* https://www.thenationalnews.com/business/economy/2022/09/19/new-uae-initiative-aims-to-double-family-businesses-contribution-to-gdp-to-320bn-by-2032/

Cano-Rubio, M., Fuentes-Lombardo, G., & Vallejo-Martos, M. C. (2017). Influence of the lack of a standard definition of "family business" on researcher into their international strategies. *European Research on Management and Business Economics, 23*, 132–146.

Churchill, N. C., & Hatten, K. 1. (1987). Non-market-based transfers of wealth and power: A research framework for family businesses. *American Journal of Small Business, 11*(3), 51–64.

Davis, J. (2001, July). *Definitions and typologies of the family business.* Harvard Business School Background Note, 802-007.

Davis, J., & Tagiuri, R. (1982). *The influence of life stages on father-son work relationships in family companies.* Unpublished manuscript, Graduate School of Business Administration. University of Southern California.

Donnelley, R. (1964). The family business. *Harvard Business Review, 42*(4), 93–105.

Dyer, W. G., Jr. (1986). *Cultural changes in family business: Anticipating and managing business and family transitions.* Jossey-Bass.

EY Global. (2023). How the largest family enterprises are outstripping global economic growth. *EY Global.* https://www.ey.com/en_gl/insights/family-enterprise/family-business-index

Fares, R. (2023). The future of family businesses in Lebanon. *Medium.* https://medium.com/adnarfares/the-future-of-family-businesses-in-lebanon-9f7c5f1c0fba

Fattal. (2021). A family business. *Fattal.* https://www.fattal.com.lb/the-story-of-fattal.html#a-family-business

Forbes. (2024). Top 100 Arab family businesses 2024. *Forbes.* https://www.forbesmiddleeast.com/lists/top-100-arab-family-businesses-2024/fattal-group/

International Trade Centre. (2020). Promoting SME competitiveness in Zambia. *International Trade Centre.* https://www.zda.org.zm/wp-content/uploads/2020/10/Zambia-Competiveness-Survey.pdf

Konge, W. (2014, February 19). A look at Ranchod family business legacy. *Times of Zambia.* https://www.times.co.zm/?p=10457

Lansberg, I. S., Perrow, E. L., & Rogolsky, S. (1988). Family business as an emerging field. *Family Business Review, 1*(1), 1–8.

Leach, P., Kenway-Smith, W., Hart, A., Morris, T., Ainsworth, J., Beterlsen, E., Iraqi, S., & Pasari, V. (1990). *Managing the family business in the UK. A Stoy Hayward survey in conjunction with the London Business School.* Stoy Hayward.

Mafatlal, P. (2023, February 12). Family businesses – Leading the 'Make in India' movement. *Times of India.* https://timesofindia.indiatimes.com/blogs/voices/family-businesses-leading-the-make-in-india-movement/

Magasi, C. (2016). Factors influencing business succession planning among SMes in Tanzania. *European Journal of Business and Management, 8*(3), 126–135.

McClatchie, C. (2023, November 23). Why Japan is home to the world's oldest businesses. *CEO Magazine.* https://www.theceomagazine.com/business/management-leadership/japan-oldest-businesses/

Miller, E. J., & Rice, A. K. (1967). *Systems of organizations.* Tavistock.

Pieper, T., Kellermanns, F., & Astrachan, J. (2021). Update 2021: Family businesses' contribution to the U.S. economy. *Family Enterprise.* https://familyenterpriseusa.com/wp-content/uploads/2021/02/Family-Businesses-Contribution-to-the-US-Economy_v.01272021-FINAL_4.pdf

Puri-Mirza, A. (2021). Private sector establishments numbers UAE 2016-2020. *Statista.* https://www.statista.com/statistics/1148078/uae-number-of-private-sector-establishments/#:~:text=In%202020%2C%20the%20total%20number,compared%20to%20the%20previous%20year

PwC. (2023, December 15). *PwC's 11th Indian family business survey: Transform to build trust and grow.* PwC. https://www.pwc.in/services/entrepreneurial-and-private-business/11th-family-business-survey-2023-india-report.html

SiliconIndia. (2014, February 10). India's 10 oldest family owned businesses. *SiliconIndia.* https://www.siliconindia.com/news/business/indias-10-oldest-family-owned-businesses-nid-161014-cid-3.html

Statista Mobility Market Insights. (2022). Porche Report 2022. https://www.statista.com/study/60891/porsche-report/

Stern, M. H. (1986). *Inside the family-held business.* Harcourt Brace Jovanovich.

Tharawat, M. (2023, October 12). Economic impact of family businesses – A compilation of facts. *Tharawat Magazine Orbis Terra Media.* https://www.tharawat-magazine.com/facts/economic-impact-family-businesses/

The National. (2023, March 25). Sheikh Mohammed establishes centre to support family businesses in Dubai. *National NOW Times.* https://www.thenationalnews.com/uae/government/2023/02/02/sheikh-mohammed-establishes-centre-to-support-family-businesses-in-dubai/

The Wadia Group. (2010). The Wadia Group. *Wadia Group.* https://www.wadiagroup.com/wadia_group.html#verticalTab2

Varghese, J. (2021). UAE: How did family businesses come about and how are they structured? Family business play a huge role in the Gulf region – But how do they operate? *Your Money.* https://gulfnews.com/your-money/expert-columns/uae-how-did-family-businesses-come-about-and-how-are-they-structured-1.1619001837624

Walmart. (2023). How many people work at Walmart? *Walmart.* https://corporate.walmart.com/askwalmart/how-many-people-work-at-walmart

Zeidan, F. (2021). *Family business in Lebanon: Leadership practices and continuity.* Doctoral dissertation, Hungarian University of Agriculture and Life Sciences. Hungarian University of Agriculture and Life Sciences. https://phd.mater.uni-mate.hu/99/1/1624969841-firas_zeidan_dissertation_08-06-2021-final_vb5_DOI.pdf

Chapter 3

England: The Warm Age Wood Company

Antoinette Flynn

University of Limerick, Ireland

Introduction

This is a 'hearth'-warming story of a family business called the *Warm Age Wood Company (WAWC)*, combating fuel poverty in their remote rural locality by warming the hearths of those in need in Teesdale, County Durham, Northern England, United Kingdom (UK). Fuel poverty is a poverty of the developed world, the crux of which is the lack of affordability, whereas energy poverty is an accessibility issue for the developing world (Halkos & Aslanidis, 2023). In Europe, evidence of the greatest rise in fuel poverty is in homes in the West of Europe, where fuel poverty has reached 26% (Halkos & Aslanidis, 2023). Three factors influence whether a household is experiencing fuel poverty: household income, household energy requirements and fuel prices (Durham Insight, 2022). A 'fuel poor' household is one where the energy costs of maintaining a sustaining health and well-being indoor environment are beyond the householder's economic reach. When the cost of heating a home pushes the residents under the official poverty line, either because of a low energy efficiency property or low incomes or a combination of both, then they are deemed to be fuel poor, as defined by the United Kingdom's Department of Energy Security and Net Zero (2024).[1] In the County of Durham, Northern England, where this family business is located, 11.5% of households are in fuel poverty (Durham Insight, 2022).

The *WAWC* co-founders, husband and wife team Geraldine O'Connor (Company Secretary) and Dave Watson (Director) operated their family business with one of their four sons,[2] Tom Watson (Director), as a social enterprise or otherwise known as a community interest company, by providing free/subsidised wood briquettes for those in fuel poverty from August 2014 to February 2023 (Hartley, 2014; The Warm Age Wood Company, 2014). The Watson family

---

[1]A household is in fuel poverty as defined by the UK Government, when its fuel poverty energy efficiency rating is Band D or below and their disposable income after housing and fuel costs is below the poverty line (Department of Energy Security and Net Zero, 2024).
[2]Their four sons are Tom, Ben, Taigh and Finn.

Attaining the 2030 Sustainable Development Goal of No Poverty, 27–39
Copyright © 2025 Antoinette Flynn
Published under exclusive licence by Emerald Publishing Limited
doi:10.1108/978-1-83608-570-620241003

demonstrated socially responsible leadership by being agents of social change in their community, harnessing the help of those around them, to support those in most need. Fitzgerald et al. (2010) identified similar community leadership roles adopted by other socially minded business owners, pursuing 'solutions to neglected problems' in economically vulnerable communities (Santos, 2012, p. 335). Researchers have shown that family businesses that exhibit socially responsible behaviours like the *WAWC*, do so along three dimensions: (i) community commitment, (ii) community support and (iii) a sense of community (Kurland & McCaffrey, 2020; Niehm et al., 2008). This *WAWC* case study is a classic example of how family businesses can bring communities together along those three community dimensions to conquer (fuel) poverty, contributing to the sustainability and well-being of their small, rural community.

Products and Services Offered by *WAWC*

The *WAWC* provided quality, carbon-neutral, sustainable wood and bark briquettes, and hand-knitted and crocheted merchandise. The company sold dry, sustainable wood briquette products for home fires, where the briquettes were created from the offcuts of furniture-making waste and construction waste (Hartley, 2014). As part of their family business, they supported the vulnerable in the community across a 25-mile radius through their '10-2-1 promise.' 10 means that for every 10 briquette packs sold, the company provided 1 free/subsidised pack to identified fuel-vulnerable individuals.

Their business model was dually funded by their normal trade in briquettes for solid fuel stoves and secondly, through the sale of knitwear, created by a community of volunteer knitters (see Fig. 3.1). The knitwear was sold in their WAWC shop to fund the purchase of briquettes for distribution to those in fuel poverty to underpin their 10-2-1 commitment. This business enabled the provision of an estimated 840 tonnes of fuel to those in need from 2014 to 2022 (Watson, 2024).

The value of WAWC to the community was recognised and supported by other businesses, who generously donated to support the costs of purchasing the

Fig. 3.1.   Dave Watson and Geraldine O'Connor Holding Briquettes and Knitting in Front of Their Fire. *Source:* Provided by the Warm Age Wood Company.

wool, including GSK, The Bowes Museum, Teesdale U3A, Persimmon Homes Durham, Centrica among others (Centrica, 2014; Southen, 2015). How did the team identify those in need? The business relied on a network of community organisations to support them by providing referrals. The referrals came from senior day clubs, food banks, money advice centres and other organisations that support the disabled or unemployed as well as WAWC's own efforts identifying those in the community with a clear need through the personalised fuel delivery service (Watson, 2024).

The WAWC family business was formally recognised in several ways. Centrica (an energy and services company) recognised the good that WAWC did, and the company was the 2014 winner of The Big Energy Idea sponsored by Ignite and Centrica. The WAWC received £25,000 seed funding in March 2015 from the impact investment fund called Ignite Social Enterprise (Centrica, 2014). In 2016, the WAWC was also a finalist in Teesdale Business Awards under the category of 'Best Community Engagement Company', and in 2019, WAWC was the winner of the 'Social Responsibility' award at the 2019 Teesdale Business Awards (Northern Echo, 2020) and winner of the Good Neighbour Award, 2019 as shown below (Fig. 3.2) in the Warm Age Wood shop front (Watson, 2024).

Fig. 3.2.   2019 Good Neighbour Award in the Window of the Warm Age Wood Shop. *Source:* Provided by the Warm Age Wood Company.

The Durham Region

Why did this family business/social enterprise with a focus on fuel poverty manifest in County Durham? County Durham is very rural with a low population density, compared to the rest of the country (Darby, 2024, p. 12). There is a lack of public transport which inhibits access to services, education and employment. The cost of travel and long journey times have also acted as barriers to connectivity and compound poverty, especially in the remote rural parts of Durham (Darby, 2024). 'People living in the Durham Dales can often live miles from their nearest neighbour, and many are on low incomes,' said Geraldine (MacFarlane, 2015, p. 1). Country Durham is also at risk of worsening poverty and fuel poverty due to the quality of employment available in the area, which is low paid, irregular hours and not steady (Darby, 2024).

Without a doubt, fuel poverty exacerbates the negative impacts on people's health and well-being that result from prolonged periods without sufficient warmth or other domestic energy services (Bridgen & Robinson, 2023). In this part of the world, the older houses, which were built long ago for the mining workers, are difficult to keep warm due to their lack of insulation. Unfortunately, that infrastructure problem of cold homes combined with lower-than-average national incomes in this area are the catalysts for a higher than national average number of cold-related deaths in Durham County, due to an increased risk of cardiovascular disease, respiratory illnesses and stroke (Durham County Council, 2014; Watson, 2024).

A long-term solution to fuel poverty is tackling the poor-quality housing stock in the United Kingdom, especially in rural areas. The *Warm Front* programme in England (2000–2013) resulted in 2.3 million 'fuel poor' homes receiving energy efficiency upgrades to save the households money on fuel (an average extra annual income of £1,894.79 per participating household) and had recorded related health improvements. This programme reduced the incidence of fuel poverty and had the beneficial effect of reducing greenhouse gas emissions (Sovacool, 2015). These infrastructural programmes are undoubtedly impactful but costly, and they do not alleviate fuel poverty's immediate and pressing misery. The WAWC saw this social and economic need in County Durham and marshalled its resources to support those in fuel poverty through social cooperation and creativity.

Vision and Mission of the WAWC

The mission of the WAWC was to keep people warm and well and to preserve their local beautiful environment. Their social value creation was enshrined in their motto of 'warm homes, warm bodies and warm hearts', a philosophy shining through their 10-2-1 commitment, their appealing, cosy knitted products and their inclusive business model (The Warm Age Wood Company, 2014). This family-run social enterprise directed their social mission towards the welfare enhancement of their local community, specifically to benefit those suffering under the yoke of fuel poverty, which is in line with the SDG#1 eradicating poverty (Owen et al., 2015). There is possible tension in a family-run social enterprise between the owning family's role as a benefactor and its role as a beneficiary (Randolph et al., 2022), which can be resolved by the transgenerational united values and common belief in the greater good, held by Dave, Geraldine and their son Tom.

Background to the WAWC Family and the Business

Research has shown that small businesses in rural areas in Scotland, Northern Ireland, Wales, Northeast of England, Yorkshire and Humber are more likely to have a social mission and be deemed social enterprises (Liñares-Zegarra & Wilson, 2022). However, few family businesses explicitly set goals for social impact, and none surveyed by PriceWaterhouseCoopers make those goals their top priority in a global survey of family businesses (PriceWaterhouseCoopers, 2023). This survey also highlighted how family businesses who are engaging with their stakeholders is changing and environmental, social, governance, diversity and inclusion issues are now at the forefront. In short, a family business with an explicit social mission is a rarity and none is so rare or precious than the WAWC.

WAWC, as a social enterprise, is the combination of entrepreneurship and social outreach (Rey-Martí et al., 2016); a business that engages in entrepreneurial activities with a social mission (Bosma & Levie, 2010). The raison d'être of WAWC was to have a social impact by supporting vulnerable people through the reduction of fuel poverty and simultaneously, operate a sustainable business model applying free market principles, a true social enterprise (Alter, 2007; Battilana & Dorado, 2010; Yunus, 2009). Are family businesses compatible with the ethos of a social enterprise? Long and Mathews (2011) argued that the nature of family-owned businesses makes them uniquely suited to social exchange and reciprocity, grounded in the family businesses' ethical structures. These characteristics influenced the development of non-economic goals, strong interpersonal relationships and cross-generational sustainability. In that light, the WAWC, as a family-owned social enterprise directed by socially conscious and socially active family members, was ideally suited to deliver respite for those suffering fuel poverty in the Durham Dales region.

Former teacher, Dave Watson, former healthcare worker, Geraldine O'Connor and their son Tom Watson, social activist, 'focused on trying to make the world a better place' (Watson, 2024, p. 1) are the family behind the WAWC social enterprise (Hartley, 2014; Watson, 2014). The business was started with just GBP 102 capital and a wealth of community connections and knowledge (Watson, 2024). A Scottish man, Dave as a Director of this social enterprise, had previous experience with Health Squared (Wellness and Fitness Services) and as a Senior Manager with Durham County Council (Warm Age Wood Company, 2014). His prior experiences were in public health and social services support in complex settings, which introduced him to the vulnerable in the Durham Dales community who needed support and to the social care, medical, educational and mental health professionals in the locality (Watson, 2014).

While Dave and Geraldine were the heart of WAWC, according to Tom, the three of them worked together to identify and support those vulnerable to fuel poverty. In the rural areas around Barnard Castle, many older properties were off the energy supply grid. This remoteness brought with it a range of complex needs including loneliness and isolation, which Tom says really impacted the community's wellbeing. By being actively part of the community, WAWC were often among the first to witness social issues before they became apparent to policymakers. The decision to set up a permanent retail shop for the WAWC proved integral to the core mission of WAWC. The shop acted as a hub for all that was WAWC, with a welcome for anyone that needed a chair to get warm, to have a chat and to reconnect.

It embodied the true meaning of a 'Warm Space' well before it became normalised (Lowe, 2022). It was often through the interactions in the WAWC shop that Dave and Geraldine were alerted to individual needs, sometimes more complex and evolving than fuel deprivation. The volunteer knitters, known as *the Warm Age Woolly Warmers*, met in the shop to swap ideas, share skills and socialise with those that shared their purpose, in a sense their tribe. Very sadly, Dave died of pancreatic cancer in late 2017 (Paul, 2018) and after Dave's untimely passing, Tom and Geraldine continued the WAWC business until the onset of the COVID-19 pandemic made their business activities very difficult.

SDG#1 No Poverty and the WAWC

SDG#1 aims to eradicate poverty in all its forms and dimensions by 2030, promoting shared prosperity and social inclusion (United Nations, 2015, p. 41). Poverty is a complex, multidimensional problem encompassing social, economic, cultural and political factors. Fuel poverty, as an aspect of deprivation, is also complex and driven by multiple social and spatial dimensions (Middlemiss & Gillard, 2015). Therefore, poverty eradication must be grounded in inclusivity to break down structural inequalities and systemic barriers in a sustainable and multigenerational impactful manner.

By targeting fuel poverty in Durham Dales, the WAWC directly addressed SDG#1 by providing free/subsidised fuel for those in poverty and more specifically targets SDG#1.1 aiming to eradicate extreme poverty for all people and SDG#1.a by actively mobilising the local community resources to address local fuel poverty arising from poverty in a meaningful and immediate way. By focusing on the local nature of their customer base, the WAWC deliberately developed their understanding of and trust within the community to better identify those in fuel poverty, who may have other complex needs: as Geraldine said, 'the notion of being local is fundamental to us' (Conner, 2014, p. 12). Tom explained that a visit to a remote location in Durham to deliver firewood may have resulted in additional physical and emotional supports being identified and resolved, like repairing a door or taking the time to connect, among others (Watson, 2014). While Tom admitted that the business model wasn't perfect, it had an agility and connectivity that larger organisations would struggle to develop and that capacity 'fuelled' the success of WAWC to reduce this specific, pressing poverty in this part of the world (Watson, 2014).

Reporting and Measurement: Metrics for SDG#1 Success

As part of the operation of WAWC, specific information was gathered to monitor the company's performance in relation to their mission of 'warm homes, warm bodies and warm hearts.' This information was also useful when the company was applying for funding, sponsorship and awards. According to figures provided by WAWC, some of the key annual metrics recorded and collated included the number of houses kept warm, carbon emissions saved through direct activities, community outreach, local beneficiaries including the knitting community and suppliers engaged with during activities (Watson, 2024). One caveat here is that some of the data collection ends in 2018 as the family business adjusted to the passing of its co-founder, Dave Watson.

The number of homes kept warm in the winter months from 2014 to 2022 was on average 23 homes per annum, with a peak of 34 homes in 2018. This is clear evidence that through its community engagement business model, WAWC addressed fuel poverty in its locality. The other metrics indicate that poverty reduction was not the only accomplishment of this social enterprise. As part of the information gathered annually, the founders consciously recorded the impact the family business had on the environment in terms of CO_2 emissions saved (their carbon performance) due to their direct activities, compared to what would have happened without this organisation, as shown in Fig. 3.3. As the activity in the company increased, it was matched by a rising carbon performance, albeit data are only available up to 2018. From 2014 to 2018, the average ratio of carbon emissions saved per homes released from fuel poverty was 1.75 tonnes per home, but it stabilised to approximately 2 tonnes per home from 2015–2018. This consistent carbon performance illustrates a social enterprise doing good in multiple ways!

CO_2 Tonnes Saved

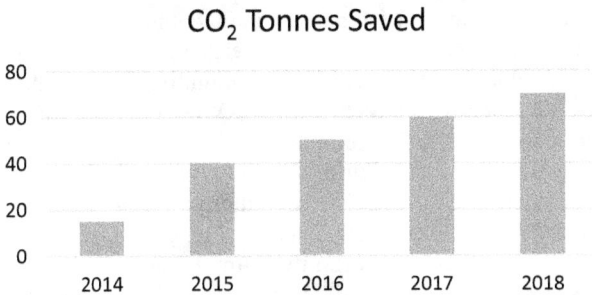

Fig. 3.3. The Annual Carbon Performance of the Warm Age Wood Company. *Source:* Data provided by the Warm Age Wood Company.

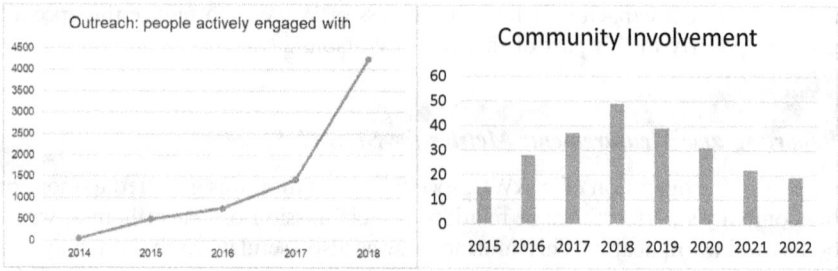

Fig. 3.4.   The Number of People the Warm Age Wood Company
Engaged With on a Yearly Basis. *Source:* Data provided by the Warm Age
Wood Company.

The WAWC actively spread the word of their mission and business model
through engagement with the public at their weekly market stalls, their online
presence and the physical shop in Barnard Castle. This outreach engagement activity
is estimated and shown in Fig. 3.4, but the figures may be conservative, according to
Tom, as they do not fully capture the public engagement attributed to the network of
knitters, and wider interested community (Watson, 2024). In tandem with WAWC's
publicity garnered from multiple awards and funding successes, their outreach
activity exposed the plight of fuel poverty in the Durham Dales and its associated
negative health consequences to local and national policymakers and other stakeholders. This level of outreach engagement allowed WAWC to consistently showcase how they, as a small family business, mobilised their various resources, through
funding sponsorship, business activities and with the collaboration of the volunteer
community of knitters, to implement their business model to end fuel poverty for
those in need in the Durham Dales (Fig. 3.4).

Community involvement is central to the success of the WAWC's mission. The
volunteer knitters group began in 2014, a brainchild of Geraldine (Conner, 2014)
and steadily grew in numbers. In 2015, there was a community of 15 knitters who
sold over 500 knitted items to customers from 20 countries. Special knitted items
commissioned included hats for patients undergoing chemotherapy and special
wool socks for the elderly (Watson, 2024). Community involvement also extended
to primary school children and in 2015 the WAWC knitters taught more than 60
primary school-goers to knit. The community of knitters peaked at 49 in 2018 but
managed to remain at about 20 during the COVID-19 pandemic era despite the
public health restrictions (see Fig. 3.4, community involvement).

Based on these metrics, the WAWC achieved its goal of reducing fuel poverty
in its local area and more importantly with its limited financial resources,
managed to harness the goodwill and talents of the local community towards that
goal. In the process, it brought public awareness to the plight of fuel poverty, gave
a community of artisans a joint social purpose and increased the well-being of all
involved.

Business and Greater Good

WAWC's goal was to improve Durham people's well-being, by reducing fuel poverty through their 10-2-1 promise and funding fuel via community knitting (Conner, 2014). The Durham Dales area has a strong knitting heritage, with historical records showing that coal miners knitted on the journey between the mines and smelting areas, supplementing their income in the 19th century (Hartley, 2014). Indeed, the co-founder Geraldine remembers being taught as a child by her grandmother to knit 'with six-inch nails', and she learnt more from the WAWC knitting community (Conner, 2014, p. 12). A core element of successfully achieving WAWC's goal of reducing local fuel poverty was the funding provided by the local network of knitters, who volunteered their time, skills and care to produce knitwear for sale. The Warm Age Woolly Warmers produced hats, mittens, gloves, dog coats, woolly vests, cardigans, jumpers, tea cosies and socks to raise funds to buy more briquettes (Hartley, 2014).

More than a 'woollen mill', this social enterprise united the community of knitters and provided purpose and meaning to their creative pursuits. As Geraldine related to the local newspaper, Teesdale Mercury, the knitting community promoted the notion of good well-being, which is centred on 'being connected' with each other (Conner, 2014, p. 12). By purchasing the woollen items from WAWC, customers were kept warm and by extension, those vulnerable to fuel poverty were kept warm in the cold, northerly winters. Geraldine kept a log of items sold to connect the knitters and the final recipients to help knitters who aren't very mobile to connect to the beneficiaries of their generosity: 'one of our knitters has made a scarf and she knows it's been worn by a girl who loves it' (Conner, 2014, p. 12). The company stated that they 'want to connect the people who have made the woollen items with those who receive it and to be able to say to our knitters to whom and where it has gone in the world' (Warm Age Wood Company, 2014, p. 1).

The business very deliberately offered the knitting volunteers an opportunity to come together during the week to connect and share their stories, patterns and experiences while they knit, bonding over a cup of tea. This bonding extended to connections made with customers of the woollen goods, with the fuel vulnerable and with a sense of place. This nurtured community spirit brought neighbours together who sometimes lived quite a distance from each other, with a common purpose, a shared love of knitting and a willingness to contribute to the greater good. This community of knitters, aged between 8 and 80 (Conner, 2014), created their own warmth through human contact and the sense of being valued for their craft and skills (Hartley, 2014). By connecting those that volunteer with the stories of the beneficiaries of their largesse, this community embraced life-enhancing actions that contributed to their lives and communities, ultimately creating a pathway to the five steps of well-being 'Connect, Be Active, Take Notice, Keep Learning and Give', as developed by the New Economics Foundation (Public Health Agency, 2023).

These aspects of connectivity and purpose as pathways to well-being that were enshrined in the 'warm homes, warm bodies and warm hearts' WAWC mission were carefully nurtured by Dave and Geraldine, as Tom reflected that 'the causes of loneliness are not just physical isolation and lack of companionship but also sometimes the lack of a useful role in society' (Watson, 2024).

What Next for the WAWC and SDG#1?

In late 2017, when Dave Watson passed away from pancreatic cancer, WAWC continued in honour of his memory (Smiley Movement, 2019). Retail sales peaked in 2017 at £14,890, took a dip in 2018 and bounced back in 2019 to £12,837 (Watson, 2024). In 2020, the world faced an unprecedented pandemic that challenged every aspect of modern life, including WAWC whose sales fell to £5,912 in 2020. During the COVID-19 pandemic, Geraldine announced 'we have taken the decision to close the Warm Age shop in Barnard Castle permanently', as the family business was unable to ensure everyone's safety in the shop due to the pandemic (Teesdale Mercury, 2020). Also, the rent for the WAWC shop was the largest operational expense for the family business and without regular activity, keeping the shop open was no longer viable (Watson, 2024). The shop closed but the community organisation continued with its promise to fuel *warm homes, warm bodies and warm hearts* (Teesdale Mercury, 2020).

The business looked for alternative ways of selling their knitted products, and it continued to provide wool for those who wished to knit. WAWC announced that it will continue to 'deliver briquettes, sell the remaining knitted stock and provide wool for those who wish to continue to knit' (The Warm Age Wood Company, 2020, p.1). Geraldine thanked 'everyone who has made the shop such a wonderfully warm place to be; to the volunteers who helped run the shop, the knitters who filled it with such wonderful colours and to everyone who ever bought anything, and to those who came and sat and talked, thank you' (Teesdale Mercury, 2020, p. 1). The WAWC volunteer knitting groups continued to meet at pre-organised satellite locations (usually cafes), financially sponsored by WAWC. This approach didn't always work well as it lacked the flexibility that these volunteers needed, which previously the WAWC shop gave them. It is a testament to the strength of WAWC, which enabled these networks of volunteers to be able to continue to meet despite the logistical issues. WAWC as a socially responsible family business, truly embodied community commitment, community support and a sense of community (Kurland & McCaffrey, 2020; Niehm et al., 2008).

In the face of many challenges, including lack of sufficient funding, continuous efforts to identify the fuel poor and deliver their 10-2-1 promise, co-ordination of the knitting network and its activities and the death of a co-founder/husband/father, this wonderful family social enterprise persisted in addressing fuel poverty in their beloved Durham Dales until an unprecedented global pandemic finally resulted in the WAWC winding down. While WAWC achieved its goal of 'warm homes, warm bodies and warm hearts', its greatest achievement was to shine a light on fuel poverty. Fuel poverty is now actively monitored in Durham via the Fuel Poverty Dashboard (Durham Insight, 2022) and local government (Darby, 2024).

In the United Kingdom, roughly three quarters of public money spent on energy poverty policy interventions fails to reach those that are fuel poor

(Boardman, 2013). Family businesses like WAWC operating in the private sphere address this often hidden and intractable social problem in an immediate and impactful way, while also having a positive influence on the well-being of the stakeholders involved. Funding and supporting local social enterprises like WAWC are important ways governments can tackle this insidious form of poverty while inspiring social cohesion and well-being. Certainly, the ethos of 'warm homes, warm bodies and warm hearts' has had a transformational impact on the Durham Dales community and is truly an inspirational legacy for Dave Watson, RIP.

References

Alter, K. (2007). *A social enterprise typology*. Virtue Ventures LLC. http://www.4lenses.org/setypology

Battilana, J., & Dorado, S. (2010). Building sustainable hybrid organizations: The case of commercial microfinance organizations. *Academy of Management Journal*, *53*(6), 1419–1440.

Boardman, B. (2013). *Fixing fuel poverty: challenges and solutions*. Routledge.

Bosma, N., & Levie, J. (2010). *Global entrepreneurship monitor: 2009 global report*. Babson College, Universidad Del Desarrollo, Reykjavik University.

Bridgen, P., & Robinson, C. (2023). A decade of fuel poverty in England: A spatio-temporal analysis of needs-based targeting of domestic energy efficiency obligations. *Energy Research & Social Science*, *101*, 103139.

Centrica. (2014, December 8). Ignite investment: a family business tackling fuel poverty. *Centrica*. https://www.centrica.com/media-centre/news/2014/ignite-investment-a-family-business-tackling-fuel-poverty/

Conner, R. (2014, January 22). Woolly warmers helping to keep the cold at bay [News]. *Teesdale Mercury*, 12.

Darby, P. (2024). Poverty issues annual report. *Durham City Council*. https://democracy.durham.gov.uk/documents/s185047/Poverty%20Issues%20Annual%20Report%20-%20Cabinet%2014.02.24%20Final__.pdf

Department of Energy Security and Industrial Strategy Net Zero. (2024, April 25). *Fuel poverty statistics collection*. https://www.gov.uk/government/collections/fuel-poverty-statistics#2023-statistics

Durham County Council. (2014). NHS and public health reform. *Durham City Council*. https://democracy.durham.gov.uk/documents/s36931/NHS+Reforms.pdf

Durham Insight. (2022, May 16). Fuel poverty. *Durham Insight*. https://www.durhaminsight.info/fuel-poverty/

Fitzgerald, M. A., Haynes, G. W., Schrank, H. L., & Danes, S. M. (2010). Socially responsible processes of small family business owners: Exploratory evidence from the national family business survey. *Journal of Small Business Management*, *48*(4), 524–551.

Halkos, G., & Aslanidis, P. (2023). Addressing multidimensional energy poverty implications on achieving sustainable development. *Energies*, *16*(9), 3805.

Hartley, S. (2014, November 27). Social entrepreneurs: Family business tackling fuel poverty. *The Guardian*. https://www.theguardian.com/small-business-network/2014/nov/27/social-entrepreneurs-family-busines-fuel-poverty

Kurland, N. B., & McCaffrey, S. J. (2020). Community socio-emotional wealth: Preservation, succession, and farming in Lancaster County, Pennsylvania. *Family Business Review, 33*(3), 244–264.

Liñares-Zegarra, J. M., & Wilson, J. (2022). SMEs as social enterprises: Regional disparities, access to finance, strategic intentions, and the COVID-19 pandemic. *Enterprise Research Centre (ERC) Research Paper 97.* https://www.enterprise research.ac.uk/wp-content/uploads/2022/05/ERC-ResPap97-SMEs-as-Social-Enterprises-Linares-Zegarra-Wilson-New.pdf

Long, R. G., & Mathews, K. M. (2011). Ethics in the family firm: Cohesion through reciprocity and exchange. *Business Ethics Quarterly, 21*(2), 287–308.

Lowe, M. (2022). A warm welcome: Setting up a warm space in your community. https://www.cilip.org.uk/page/warmspaces2022

MacFarlane, K. (2015, October 26). Company donates money to tackle fuel poverty. *The Northern Echo.* https://www.thenorthernecho.co.uk/news/13896181.company-donates-money-to-tackle-fuel-poverty/

Middlemiss, L., & Gillard, R. (2015). Fuel poverty from the bottom-up: Characterising household energy vulnerability through the lived experience of the fuel poor. *Energy Research & Social Science, 6*, 146–154.

Niehm, L. S., Swinney, J., & Miller, N. J. (2008). Community social responsibility and its consequences for family business performance. *Journal of Small Business Management, 46*(3), 331–350.

Northern Echo. (2020, February 13). Who won the prizes at the Teesdale Business Awards? *Northern Echo.*

Owen, F., Li, J., Whittingham, L., Hope, J., Bishop, C., Readhead, A., & Mook, L. (2015). Social return on investment of an innovative employment option for persons with developmental disabilities: Common ground co-operative. *Nonprofit Management and Leadership, 26*(2), 209–228.

Paul, M. (2018, March 10). Bike ride in memory of man who brought warmth to Teesdale. *Teesdale Mercury.* https://www.teesdalemercury.co.uk/news/bike-ride-in-memory-of-man-who-brought-warmth-to-teesdale

PriceWaterhouseCooper (PwC). (2023). Transform to build trust – PwC's 11th Global Family Business Survey. www.pwc.com/familybusinesssurvey

Public Health Agency. (2023, December). Take 5 steps to well-being leaflet. *Public Health Agency.* https://www.publichealth.hscni.net/sites/default/files/2023-12/Take%205%20steps%20to%20wellbeing%20leaflet.pdf

Randolph, R. V., Alexander, B. N., Madison, K., & Barbera, F. (2022). When family business meets social enterprise: An integrative review and future research agenda. *Family Business Review, 35*(3), 219–245.

Rey-Martí, A., Ribeiro-Soriano, D., & Palacios-Marqués, D. (2016). A bibliometric analysis of social entrepreneurship. *Journal of business research, 69*(5), 1651–1655.

Santos, F. M. (2012). A positive theory of social entrepreneurship. *Journal of Business Ethics, 111*(3), 335–351.

Smiley Movement. (2019). The Warm Age Wood Company. *Smiley Movement.* https://smileymovement.org/news/the-warm-age-wood-company

Southen, L. (2015, October 22). Home fuel business boosted by cash donation. *Bdaily News.* https://bdaily.co.uk/articles/2015/10/22/home-fuel-business-boosted-by-cash-donation

Sovacool, B. K. (2015). Fuel poverty, affordability, and energy justice in England: Policy insights from the arm front program. *Energy, 93*, 361–371.

Teesdale Mercury. (2016, October 20). Social enterprise Warm Age Wood Company moves into Barnard Castle town centre shop. *Teesdale Mercury*. https://teesdalemercury.blogspot.com/2016/10/social-enterprise-warm-age-wood-company.html

Teesdale Mercury. (2020, November 22). Shop closes but community organisation still promises 'warm hearts and warm homes' [News]. *Teesdale Mercury*, p. 1. https://www.teesdalemercury.co.uk/news/shop-closes-but-community-organisation-still-promises-warm-hearts-and-warm-homes

The Warm Age Wood Company. (2020, September 15). *Dear warm age friends* (p. 1) [Posts]. Facebook. https://www.facebook.com/warmagecic

The Warm Age Wood Company. (2014). LinkedIn profile. https://www.linkedin.com/company/the-warm-age-wood-company/?originalSubdomain=uk

United Nations. (2015). *Transforming our world: The 2030 agenda for sustainable development* (Vol. 1, p. 41). United Nations, Department of Economic and Social Affairs.

Watson, D. (2014). LinkedIn profile. https://www.linkedin.com/in/dave-watson-82364b94/

Watson, T. C. (2024). LinkedIn profile. https://www.linkedin.com/in/tomcampbellwatson/

Yunus, M. (2009). Creating a world without poverty: Social business and the future of capitalism. *Global Urban Development, 4*(2), 1–19.

Chapter 4

Zambia: SBM

Sylvia B. Mwansa[a], Brian Gregory[b] and Allan Discua Cruz[b]

[a]SBM Investments Limited, Zambia
[b]Lancaster University Management School, UK

Introduction

Simply Best Merchandise (SBM) Investments Limited, founded in 1994, is a family-owned business enterprise belonging to the Mwansa family in Zambia. Recognising the importance of entrepreneurship in economic growth and poverty reduction, SBM provides targeted coaching and mentoring from their 30 years of experience to aspiring entrepreneurs in Zambia. By assisting individuals in developing a business mindset, refining their business ideas and providing guidance on various entrepreneurial skills, SBM helps aspiring entrepreneurs navigate the challenges of starting and sustaining successful businesses. This support can lead to job creation, economic growth and ultimately poverty reduction linked to SDG#1.

SBM started in 1994 at a 60 sqm shop outlet and two members of staff at the Carousel Shopping Centre on the periphery of Lusaka's central business district. The business started as a partnership between Dr. Sylvia B. Mwansa and business colleague Anne Shinondo on a 50%–50% shareholding. After the original founders parted ways amicably, the 50% stake of Anne Shinondo was distributed as follows: Dr. Sylvia B. Mwansa as the principal shareholder with 50% equity, followed by Dr. Stephen Mwansa 10%, Mutale F. Mwansa 10%, Sampa S. Mwansa 10%, Chileshe Stephen Mwansa 10% and Kanyanta Theresa Mwansa 10%. The shareholders also became the inaugural Board of Directors, with Dr Stephen Mwansa as Chairman, and the rest being members of the Board. Regarding management, Dr Sylvia B. Mwansa (being the business's vision carrier) was appointed Chief Executive Officer, a position she still holds up to now.

The business grew proportionally with the Mwansa offspring who developed the businesses linked to personal fashion interests (e.g. getting married and having children provided new ideas about customer needs). The business expanded into a multi-shop up-market boutique in three shopping centres in Zambia: Lusaka Hotel Annex, Woodgate House and Chester House in Lusaka's CBD. In 1999 SBM What's New Boutique later became one of the pioneer shops at the first fully

Attaining the 2030 Sustainable Development Goal of No Poverty, 41–53
Copyright © 2025 Sylvia B. Mwansa, Brian Gregory and Allan Discua Cruz
Published under exclusive licence by Emerald Publishing Limited
doi:10.1108/978-1-83608-570-620241004

integrated shopping mall in Lusaka (Manda Hill Shopping Centre) merchandising office and functional wear. The business grew in terms of location, opening new outlets at Arcades Shopping Mall with Casual and Maternity wear (which emerged inspired by the expectation of Sylvia and Stephen's first grandchild) and Levy Business Centre with Weddings and Gifts store. As these outlets developed, Lusaka Hotel Annex, Woodgate House and Chester House outlets eventually closed due to the opportunities that new shopping malls provided. The stores provided apparel for Presidents, First Ladies, Very-Very Important Persons (VVIPs) (President and Vice President), VIPs and general members of society who simply desired the best fashion merchandise.

SBM later diversified into other business lines guided by family interests: Digital printing and advertising solutions; hotel and hospitality supplies for the tourism sector and change management training specialising in the Mindset Change Process® programme (copyright under the Patents and Companies Registration Agency (PACRA)). However, in 2008, due to challenges brought by currency exchange depreciation, fluctuations and volatility, SBM was severely impacted by the economic crisis, experiencing a deteriorating decline of the local currency value against major global currencies. In 2015, a decision was made to move out from the premier mall, Manda Hill shopping centre. The COVID-19 pandemic's effect on global and local supply chains led to the business relocating operations from outlets in malls that required rent to be paid in foreign currency into a One-Stop-Centre known as SBM Centre of Choice in the plush Woodland suburb of Lusaka. As of 2024, SBM operates in retail, manufacturing (printing, signage, sublimation and gift production) in a factory set up in Makeni and educational support sub-sectors with the SBM Training & Consulting Institute (SBM-TCI) and the Online store of SBM location in Makeni Farm residence.

From the experience gained over three decades, SBM directed all its knowledge into providing business solutions to individuals and institutions through The SBM-TCI and through the Mindset Change Process® as a precursor to any form of training, consulting and mentorship. All other branches and departments fall under the SBM Head Office and will be referred to as SBM in this chapter.

Background to the Family and the Business

In 2020, the world was hit by the COVID-19 pandemic, which had devastating effects on communities worldwide. Zambia was no exception; poverty-stricken households faced immense challenges during this period. In June 2020, the principal Directors of SBM Investments (husband and wife) were admitted to hospital with COVID-19 and stayed for almost a month. Being in a restricted place with almost nothing to do, Sylvia was able to identify the need for a mindset shift to deal with different issues. A programme called Mindset Change had been on the drawing board for almost six years. The hospital stay allowed reviving the process for its induction. This became an imperative action point that SBM embraced as a new calling. Upon discharge from the hospital, the Mindset Change Process® programme was launched to change mindsets in homes and communities. Utilising a tool called 'My Process to Mindset Change', SBM aimed to address the specific challenges of effective, efficient, retirement preparedness and succession planning required to navigate the repercussions of the pandemic.

During the pandemic and beyond, poverty-stricken households have been disproportionately affected. SBM recognised the power of mindset change in promoting lasting solutions to ending poverty in Zambia.

Products and/or Services Offered by the Family Business

The product range offered by SBM is detailed in Table 4.1.

Table 4.1. Product Range of SBM.

• Application of Mindset Change Process® and use of Success Planner	• Cocktail Chats with Sunshine Sylvia platform for telling positive stories.
• Personal goal setting as a way of life	• The wheel of life for living a life of a total person in the six areas of life
• Marketing and selling strategies	• Etiquette and personal grooming
• Change management – That inspires entrepreneurship mindset building Plan B for financial freedom	• Corporate governance for public service, business, and not-for-profit institutions
• Retirement preparedness	• Anti-corruption strategies
• Succession planning	• Strategic leadership
• Networking for success	• Intimacy relationship building for couples and partners
• Recognition of prior learning (RPL), a Technical Education, Vocational and Entrepreneurship Training Authority (TEVETA) programme that empowers communities.	• Mindset change for peak performance of institutions to enhance productivity.
• Quality assurance facilitation to those institutions needing to start companies	• Supported entrepreneurship transition from sustainable business mentorship foundation (SBMF)

SBM: Mentorship Around the Wheel of Life

SBM and the Mindset Change Process® have played a significant role in embracing SDG#1, which aims to end poverty, across the six areas of the Wheel of Life: Family and Home, Mental and Educational, Financial and Career, Physical and Health, Social and Cultural and Spiritual and Ethical.

Family and Home

For SBM, life begins and ends with family and homemaking. The Mindset Change Process® has emphasised the importance of cleanliness and hygiene, creating behavioural changes within families and making them more conscious of their living conditions. Improved sanitation facilities and hygiene practices through SBM facilitation impact the family and home where individuals seek activities that lead to healthier living environments for families, reducing the risk of diseases and illnesses. This element aligns with SDG#1.5 by building resilience to environmental, economic and social disasters.

Mental and Educational Support

SBM has focused on propagating access to clean and safe sanitation facilities in schools, improving the overall learning environment and promoting better attendance and retention rates among students, particularly girls. The Mindset Change Process® has highlighted the significance of hygiene practices in preventing diseases, leading to increased awareness and consciousness among individuals about their health, mental health and well-being. This item aligns with SDG#1.4 linked to equal rights to ownership, basic services, technology and economic resources.

Financial and Career

This item is linked to SDG#1.b, which is associated with governments creating sound policy frameworks at the national, regional and international levels, based on pro-poor and gender-sensitive development strategies, to support accelerated investment in poverty eradication actions (United Nations, n.d.). This area is also aligned with achieving SDG#1.b.1 which targets pro-poor public social spending. Financial & Career help to consider where individuals would want to be in the next 5–10 years. The Mindset Change Process® has encouraged improved personal and community hygiene, increasing productivity and career prospects. Such focus helps shape professional careers, retirement preparedness, succession planning and customer service.

Physical and Health

SBM believes that we should nourish and exercise our bodies to help us achieve our goals in life. SBM contributes towards improved access to sanitation facilities, promoting better sanitation and hygiene practices, and reducing the prevalence of diseases, which aligns with SDG#6.2. The Mindset Change Process® addresses cultural and behavioural barriers related to sanitation practices, improving physical health outcomes. A lot of individuals do not pay attention to this spoke of the wheel of life thereby neglecting the negative impact to SDG#1. With a deliberate focus on reducing poverty, SBM believes that paying attention to Physical and Health will enhance the achievement of SDG#1.

Social and Cultural

Social (Networks) and Cultural (Values) are linked to SDG#1 as we pass on the importance of both to future generations. SBM believes that our social and cultural beliefs shape our values. Therefore, SBM focuses on community involvement, fostering a sense of collective responsibility for maintaining sanitation facilities and promoting cleanliness. The Mindset Change Process® challenges traditional attitudes and beliefs around improving sanitation increasing social acceptance and participation in sanitation initiatives.

Spiritual and Ethical

For SBM, spiritually, cleanliness is Godliness (such a statement is often attributed to John Wesley). SBM believes that the concept of cleanliness as Godliness can be applied to several areas that align with the UN SDGs. For example, SDG#6 (Clean Water and Sanitation) contends that cleanliness plays a critical role in achieving this goal by ensuring access to clean water and proper sanitation facilities, promoting hygiene practices, and preventing waterborne diseases. As SDG#3 relates to Good Health and Well-being, it links to personal hygiene, healthcare settings and living environments to prevent the spread of diseases and improve overall well-being. The Mindset Change Process® puts forward that spiritual alignment and ethical behaviour are a cornerstone of humanity which links to living a life as if someone is looking.

Vision and Mission

Mission

> We help you see the world differently; discover opportunities you
> may never have imagined and achieve results that bridge what is,
> with what can be.

Vision

To be the premier service provider in motivating and developing people to their full potential through effective personal time management and change management solutions.

Clients of SBM include individuals seeking personal growth and self-improvement; corporate organisations aiming to enhance employee productivity and well-being; government agencies and non-profit organisations focused on community development; entrepreneurs and small business owners looking to enhance their leadership and management skills and anyone looking to transform their mindset and improve their overall quality of life. Well-structured mindset change training provided by SBM aims to bring success to clients by helping them apply modern change management methods, starting with a balanced and or harmonised self through the Wheel of Life.

SDG#1: SBM and Poverty Reduction

SBM is closely aligned with the United Nations Sustainable Development Goal #1 (SDG#1) of reducing poverty. The organisation's commitment to mindset changes and empowerment directly contributes to SDG#1, and its efforts resonate with specific targets and indicators of this goal. SBM's vision and mission to address poverty through mindset change processes and community empowerment are in line with Target 1.1 of SDG#1, which aims to eradicate extreme poverty for all people everywhere, especially those living in vulnerable situations. This is evidenced by the organisation's initiative to implement the Mindset Change Process® Programme to grassroots in Zambia, among others, recognising the devastating effects of poverty on these communities.

Furthermore, SBM's implementation of the 'My Process to Mindset Change®' tool directly supports SDG#1.4, which seeks to ensure that all men and women have equal rights to economic resources. By promoting efficient retirement preparedness, succession planning and entrepreneurial skills, SBM empowers individuals to access and effectively utilise economic resources, contributing to the realisation of this target.

Business Model and SDG#1

SBM is driven by a business model that revolves around promoting mindset change processes to alleviate poverty, with a specific focus on SDG#1: No Poverty. This business model consists of key elements, including awareness and education, personal development and empowerment, entrepreneurship support and collaboration with stakeholders.

One of the key elements of SBM's business model is raising awareness and providing education about the importance of mindset change in ending poverty. The organisation conducts various educational programs, workshops and seminars to ensure that individuals have the necessary information, skills and resources to overcome poverty. This aligns with SDG#1.4, which aims to ensure that individuals have access to education and resources to escape poverty.

SBM provides a variety of services. In education, SBM-TCI provides educational programs and training initiatives that are endorsed by and accredited with the Zambian Technical Education, Vocational and Entrepreneurship Training

Authority (TEVETA, the regulatory authority). The programmes empower individuals with knowledge and skills to improve their economic opportunities (aligned with SDG#1.4). By offering vocational training, entrepreneurship courses and financial literacy programs, they can equip individuals with the necessary tools to break the cycle of poverty. Through Mindset Change Process® training, the institution strives to inculcate awareness that addressing poverty requires a shift in mindset from a scarcity mentality to one that embraces possibilities and opportunities. SBM conducts workshops and seminars that challenge limiting beliefs and foster a positive and proactive mindset conducive to personal development and poverty reduction. Engaging individuals and communities in the decision-making process is crucial for sustainable poverty reduction. SBM promotes community engagement through workshops, dialogues and forums, encouraging active participation and ownership in addressing poverty-related issues. Such an approach is in line with SDG#1 (Ending poverty), SDG#3 (Good Health and Well-being), SDG#6 (Clean Water and Sanitation) and SDG#11 (Sustainable Cities and Communities).

Another key element of SBM's business model is supporting entrepreneurship. SBM provides targeted coaching and mentoring for aspiring entrepreneurs, helping them develop a business mindset, refine their business ideas and navigate the challenges of starting and sustaining successful businesses. By supporting entrepreneurship, SBM contributes to job creation and income generation in Zambia, which helps to reduce poverty. This aligns with SDG#10.2, which aims to promote the social, economic and political inclusion of all, irrespective of age, sex, disability, race, ethnicity, origin, religion or economic or other status.

Collaboration with stakeholders is also an integral part of SBM's business model. The organisation works closely with government agencies, non-profit organisations and other stakeholders working towards poverty reduction in Zambia. This collaboration enables SBM to share knowledge, resources and expertise, creating a holistic approach to addressing SDG#1.5, which aims to build the necessary partnerships for poverty eradication.

The SDG#1: 'No Poverty' serves as a guiding framework and impact measurement for SBM. The organisation's primary focus is on poverty alleviation and mindset change, but there is also a direct connection between SDG#1 and return on investment. In terms of social return on investment, SBM creates a positive impact by empowering individuals, families and communities with the necessary skills and mindsets to overcome poverty. This impact is measured in terms of improved livelihoods, increased income generation and enhanced economic opportunities. In terms of economic return on investment, SBM's activities contribute to economic growth and job creation through entrepreneurship support and business development services. By empowering aspiring entrepreneurs, SBM fosters the growth of sustainable businesses, which has a positive impact on local economies. Furthermore, SBM's focus on mindset change helps individuals develop the necessary skills, attitudes and behaviours to escape poverty and achieve sustainable development. This long-term sustainability aligns with SDG#1's goal of eradicating poverty in all its forms everywhere.

SDG#1: Poverty Reduction and SBM Stakeholders

The key stakeholders that influence SBM include government agencies, non-profit organisations, the Office of the Vice President, the Department of National Guidance and Religious Affairs, the Ministry of Labour and Social Security, local communities, and individuals and families living in poverty.

SBM trains its staff continuously and reviews training periodically to achieve SDG#1 through various methods. First, they provide education and awareness programs to staff members to ensure they understand the importance of mindset change in addressing poverty. This includes workshops and seminars on poverty alleviation and the role of mindset change in achieving sustainable development. Additionally, staff members receive training on coaching and mentoring techniques to effectively empower individuals and help them overcome self-imposed barriers. Such training equips staff members with the skills and knowledge necessary to support clients in their personal and entrepreneurial development.

The adoption of SDG#1 in SBM has had a positive impact on policymakers, especially the Ministry of Labour and Social Security who have increased their productivity levels. Before the training in Mindset Change, their executive meetings used to last five hours. The Acting Permanent Secretary confirmed that the meetings now take 1 hour 30 minutes with clear deliverables. By focusing on mindset change and empowerment, SBM has been able to uplift individuals, families and communities living in poverty. This has resulted in improved livelihoods, increased income generation and enhanced personal development for clients. The impact of SBM's programmes can be seen in the improved confidence and self-esteem of individuals, as well as the creation of successful businesses and job opportunities. By championing SDG#1, SBM has positively influenced the lives of stakeholders, providing them with the tools and support needed to break.

How Do Key Stakeholders Relate to the SDG Championed by the Organisation?

Collaboration with stakeholders is one key aspect of SBM's approach. By working with government agencies, non-profit organisations and other stakeholders dedicated to poverty reduction, SBM ensures a comprehensive and integrated approach. SBM has also partnered with the Office of the Vice President, Department of National Guidance and Religious Affairs to propagate values and principles using the Mindset Change Process® Tool. By combining efforts and expertise, SBM and its partners have developed holistic mindset change programs that align seamlessly with broader poverty alleviation initiatives in Zambia.

Stakeholders, such as government agencies and non-profit organisations, have influenced the actions of SBM related to SDG#1. By working together, stakeholders have contributed their expertise and resources to enhance the impact of SBM's programs and ensure a comprehensive approach to poverty reduction. Additionally, the partnership with the Office of the Vice President, Department of National Guidance and Religious Affairs highlights the recognition and support from the government in propagating values and principles using the Mindset

Change Process Tool. This collaboration demonstrates the influence of stake-holders on SBM's actions and their commitment to achieving SDG#1.

The partnership with the Office of the Vice President, Department of National Guidance and Religious Affairs indicates recognition and support from the government for SBM at the highest level. Engagement with the Ministry of Labour and Social Security, the Office of the Permanent Secretary and the Productivity Department has produced change agents within the Ministry and Ambassadors of the programme. This illustrates the recognition of SBM in those institutions.

Reporting and Measurement

SBM is committed to aligning its work with SDG#1, and they have implemented a range of measures to evaluate the impact of its activities against this goal. Simply providing services is not enough; SBM needs to demonstrate tangible results and improvements in the lives of the individuals they work with. One of the key indicators for SBM relates to tracking the number of individuals who have completed their mindset change programs and workshops. These programs are designed to help individuals develop a growth mindset, enhance their problem-solving abilities and improve their self-confidence. By analysing the number of individuals who have completed these programs, SBM can assess the reach and effectiveness of their efforts in empowering individuals to overcome poverty through the success stories being told by the beneficiaries of the Mindset Change Process®.

Another important indicator is the number of individuals who have started their own businesses or achieved upward mobility because of their coaching and mentoring services. By tracking these success rates, SBM can gauge their contribution to economic empowerment and the creation of sustainable livelihoods. These data also help them understand the long-term impact of their support on the economic well-being of their clients. In addition to quantitative metrics, SBM also collects qualitative feedback and testimonials from individuals who have benefited from their programs. These testimonials highlight the improvements in mindset, confidence and overall well-being experienced by their clients. By sharing these stories, SBM can provide compelling evidence of the transformative power of its services and how they are positively impacting the lives of individuals and communities.

Business and Greater Good

SBM as a business focuses on promoting mindset change and contributes to the greater good in several ways. By helping individuals and organisations shift their mindset towards positive and constructive thinking, SBM can have a transformative impact on personal, professional and societal levels. Through coaching services, SBM supports individuals in developing financial literacy, goal setting and planning skills. These tools can empower individuals to improve their financial situation, manage their resources effectively and create a pathway out of poverty. Additionally, SBM's work with organisations and communities includes training and support for entrepreneurs and small business owners, equipping them with the necessary skills and knowledge to succeed in their ventures. Furthermore, the business can collaborate with local NGOs and governmental organisations to design and implement programmes that address the root cause of poverty, such as lack of access to education, healthcare and social support systems. By raising awareness and advocating for policies that promote equitable economic opportunities, SBM contributes to reducing poverty and creating a more inclusive society. By addressing the mindset and skills needed to overcome poverty, SBM contributes to SDG#1 and helps create a world where no one is left behind.

Transformation: The services offered by SBM support individuals in developing a positive mindset, building resilience and enhancing self-awareness. These skills enable individuals to overcome challenges, cultivate a growth mindset and unlock their full potential. In doing so, individuals become better equipped to lead fulfiled lives and pursue their aspirations, leading to greater personal satisfaction and well-being and reducing poverty.

Professional Development: SBM assists organisations in fostering a positive and growth-oriented mindset among their employees. This can lead to enhanced productivity, creativity and innovation within the workplace. By helping individuals embrace change, develop effective communication skills and cultivate a positive work culture, the business can promote a more harmonious and supportive environment that drives individual and collective success.

Enhanced Interpersonal Relationships: A key aspect of mindset change is the development of emotional intelligence, empathy and effective communication skills. By promoting these skills, SBM contributes to the betterment of interpersonal relationships. Improved communication and understanding can reduce conflicts, promote collaboration and foster healthier relationships both within and outside the workplace. This, in turn, can lead to increased harmony and cooperation within families, communities and society.

Social Impact: SBM plays a significant role in promoting positive social change. By encouraging individuals and organisations to adopt a mindset focused on social responsibility, empathy and exclusivity, the business can contribute to the resolution of societal issues. For example, by promoting poverty eradication, gender equality and environmental sustainability as key values, SBM inspires individuals and organisations to actively engage in social initiatives, volunteer work and charitable activities, ultimately leading to the betterment of society through the activities e.g. promoting good values and principles with the Office of the Vice President, the Department of National Guidance and Religious affairs that promote and align to SDG#1 of no poverty.

Sustainable Development: Mindset change is crucial for driving sustainable development. By promoting a mindset focused on long-term thinking, responsible consumption and environmental consciousness, SBM can contribute to sustainable living practices. This can include raising awareness about sustainable habits such as waste reduction, energy conservation and the adoption of eco-friendly lifestyles. By educating individuals and organisations about the importance of sustainable practices, the business can contribute to the preservation of natural resources and the overall well-being of the planet.

Overall, SBM, through its focus on mindset change, has the potential to positively impact individuals, organisations and society at large. By helping individuals develop a positive and growth-oriented mindset, the business empowers individuals to lead more fulfilling lives, enhance professional success, strengthen interpersonal relationships and actively contribute to the betterment of society and the achievement of the SDGs. By promoting mindset change and personal development, the business helps individuals overcome barriers and break the cycle of poverty.

To provide benefits outside the organisation and contribute to reducing poverty (SDG#1), the family behind SBM has broad-based objectives and adopts the following approaches and strategies:

- Engage in Corporate Social Responsibility (CSR) initiatives: SBM invests in CSR activities focused on poverty reduction. This includes financial and technical assistance to impoverished communities, supporting local entrepreneurship, providing access to credit facilities, and initiating education and training programs through networks and partnerships.
- Develop inclusive procurement policies: SBM wishes to prioritise working with local suppliers and businesses from low-income regions. This can help create economic opportunities and stimulate job creation within these communities.
- Promote financial inclusion: SBM encourages and facilitates access to financial services for individuals and communities with limited resources through partnerships and networks. This may involve promoting savings and financial literacy programs and ensuring affordable, accessible banking services are available to an underprivileged population through the partnerships and networks available to SBM. In addition, SBM offers free training to individuals unable to pay, with the agreement that they can repay the fees through training remuneration once they become qualified trainers, supporting the programme's sustainability in line with SDG#1.
- Support livelihood enhancement projects: SBM partners with NGOs and development organisations to implement projects that enhance the livelihoods of marginalised communities. For example, supporting agricultural initiatives, promoting sustainable farming practices or providing vocational training for unemployed individuals to be in line with the objective of SDG#1.
- Invest in renewable energy and infrastructure: Sustainable investment in renewable energy and infrastructure projects in impoverished regions can have a transformative impact. SBM explores opportunities to fund or assist in the development of renewable energy sources, clean water projects or infrastructure projects that provide employment and improves living conditions and promotes SDG#1 towards ending poverty.
- Collaborate with other stakeholders: SBM works with governments, NGOs and other organisations involved in poverty reduction to create synergies and

maximise their impact. Collaborative efforts can lead to more comprehensive and sustainable solutions that align with SDG#1.

- Measure and report impact: SBM has established robust monitoring and evaluation mechanisms to assess the effectiveness and impact of its initiatives. Transparent reporting on their contributions towards reducing poverty fosters accountability and helps identify areas for improvement.

By adopting such approaches, SBM goes beyond its organisational boundaries and actively contributes to reducing poverty, aligning its actions with the goals of SDG#1.

Challenges of Working With SDG#1

SBM faces several challenges in effectively carrying out its programs and initiatives. One major challenge is limited resources, as securing sufficient funding and resources can be difficult. This is exacerbated by economic challenges which result in a reduced number of potential benefactors from the business community. Additionally, reaching and engaging with poverty-stricken households in remote areas with limited infrastructure poses a logistical challenge in terms of access. Changing deeply ingrained cultural and societal norms is another challenge, as some individuals may resist change or fail to see the value in mindset change. Ensuring the long-term impact and sustainability of their programmes is also a .challenge that requires ongoing support and engagement.

To address these challenges, SBM employs various strategies. One key strategy is forming partnerships with government agencies, non-profit organisations and other stakeholders to leverage resources, expertise and reach. This allows SBM to expand their reach and create a more comprehensive approach to poverty alleviation. The organisation also actively seeks funding and resources through grants and donations developing relationships with donors and stakeholders.

To address cultural and societal challenges, SBM tailors their programs to fit the specific needs and context of the communities they work with. This includes understanding and respecting local customs and traditions while challenging limiting beliefs. They also focus on raising awareness and providing educational programs to empower individuals to challenge their own beliefs and develop a growth mindset. Through workshops, seminars and coaching services, SBM equips individuals with the skills and confidence necessary for economic independence and upward mobility.

One example of success in addressing these challenges is SBM's partnership with the Ministry of Labour and Social Security which deals with productivity and directly impacts SDG#1. This collaboration allows SBM to reach a broader audience and tap into existing government structures and initiatives related to poverty reduction. By aligning their programs with the national agenda, SBM can have a more significant and sustainable impact.

What's Next for SBM and SDG#1 – Poverty Reduction

SBM's future plans concerning SDG#1 include expanding coaching services to reach more individuals and provide them with the necessary skills and mindset for income generation and entrepreneurship. SBM plans to continue organising and facilitating educational programs, workshops and seminars to raise awareness about mindset change and poverty alleviation. In addition, as a Tevet Institution, through the TEVETA programme, SBM has the Mindset Change Process® programme approved Curriculum as a National Skills Award in Zambia.

To ensure a comprehensive and integrated approach to poverty reduction, SBM collaborates with government agencies, non-profit organisations and other stakeholders. They believe that by working together, they can have a greater impact in addressing poverty in Zambia. Therefore, their plans include continuing these collaborations and exploring new partnerships and opportunities to further their impact in addressing poverty linked with SDG#1 for greater impact. Leading by example is as contained in the book *Mindset Change is Possible* (Mwansa, 2023). SBM is also developing its online presence through a website (https://www.sbmcorporateservices.com), where its success stories will be displayed.

In conclusion, and to cater for those who cannot afford the programs being offered by SBM, the Directors have registered a foundation, SBMF where those willing to support the vulnerable can partner with to alleviate poverty. Family businesses that tackle the perennial issues of poverty deal with the most vulnerable of circumstances. Family businesses like SBM call practitioners and researchers to critically examine the relevance of their actions towards others in society (Gregory et al., 2022).

References

Gregory, B., Cruz, A. D., & Jack, S. L. (2022). Critical studies in family businesses: What are we afraid of? In O. Javier Montiel Méndez, S. Tomaselli, & A. Soto Maciel (Eds.), *Family business debates: Multidimensional perspectives across countries, continents and geo-political frontiers* (pp. 51–72). Emerald Publishing Limited. https://doi.org/10.1108/978-1-80117-666-820221003

Mwansa, S. B. (2023). *Mindset change is possible.* Sotrane Publishers.

United Nations. (n.d.). *Goals 1 End poverty in all its forms everywhere.* United Nations. https://sdgs.un.org/goals/goal1#targets_and_indicators

Chapter 5

Lebanon: Fig Holding and SDG#1 No Poverty

Poh Yen Ng[a], Bettina Lynda Bastian[b] and Bronwyn Wood[c]

[a]Robert Gordon University, UK
[b]American University in Bulgaria, Bulgaria
[c]United Arab Emirates University, UAE

Introduction: Poverty in the Arab World

Poverty reduction is pivotal for sustainable development and has been identified as the first sustainability goal (SDG#1) by the United Nations. Poverty has remained a key challenge for countries in the Arab world, which is characterised by persisting levels of poverty and significant income inequalities, where the top 10% of people account for 64% of all wealth (Alvaredo et al., 2021). Arab states have undertaken diverse efforts to reduce poverty on national and regional levels to operationalise the 2030 Sustainability Agenda. Nevertheless, the achievements of objectives have been rendered difficult by numerous challenges such as ongoing regional conflicts, civil wars, political instabilities and refugee crises (mainly due to the Syrian war). Factors such as the COVID-19 pandemic and the recent Ukrainian war have also impacted food security and aggravated the poverty situation in the region (United Nations Economic and Social Commission for Western Asia [UNESCWA], 2023). Insights regarding poverty in the region come from the Multidimensional Poverty Index (MPI), which is published by the United Nations Development Programme and measures factors of living conditions that affect family spending and poverty rates, such as health, education and living standards (such as nutrition, child mortality, years of schooling, sanitation, electricity, drinking water and assets, among other factors). The MPI showed that in the aftermath of COVID-19, the Arab region experienced a significant household income loss with an extreme poverty rate of 11.3% in 2023 (UNESCWA, 2023). The pandemic has pushed eight million additional people into extreme poverty, and a total of 48 million individuals in the Arab world are now living below the poverty line (UNESCWA, 2023). The 2nd Arab multidimensional poverty report (UNESCWA, 2023) also states that the number of moderately poor people has reached 131 million of a total of 464 million inhabitants in 2023, which is an additional 22 million people compared with pre-COVID-19

Attaining the 2030 Sustainable Development Goal of No Poverty, 55–68
Copyright © 2025 Poh Yen Ng, Bettina Lynda Bastian and Bronwyn Wood
Published under exclusive licence by Emerald Publishing Limited
doi:10.1108/978-1-83608-570-620241005

times (UNESCWA, 2023). Different surveys converge in their findings that between 70% and 85% of families in non-oil-producing countries in the region have to borrow money or rely on some form of aid to cover their monthly needs, which renders them vulnerable and likely to slip into poverty (Khoury, 2019).

The present case is set in Lebanon, located in the Arab region. It describes and illustrates how Fig Holding, a family-run enterprise, has used its capabilities and resources to engage people in need and help alleviate poverty's effects on families and individuals in adverse conditions created by the economic crisis, especially after the Beirut port explosion. The case also shows how Fig Holding has transferred its knowledge to other contexts, notably Armenia, which was confronted with a refugee influx due to the military offensive in Nagorno Karabach in September 2023. The present case examines actions and initiatives adopted by a family business to achieve community engagement and support impoverished people and individuals in need during a crisis.

Fig Holding: Products and Services

Fig Holding is a portfolio company active in the culinary and hospitality industry, comprising restaurant and catering businesses around Armenian food and culture. Fig Holding consolidates different brands and business concepts all under one roof. Creating a holding company presented different advantages from an organisational perspective as it enabled the streamlining of management and provided a more cohesive approach to decision-making. It also allowed the business to share resources and expertise across its subsidiaries. Consolidating business activities under Fig Holding allowed the team to better centralise the control over the different existing and planned business entities as it streamlined decision-making and promoted a shared company culture. Table 5.1 illustrates the products and services provided by Fig Holding over the years.

Table 5.1. Timeline of Fig Holding's Companies.

Established	Name of the Business	Service or Product Summarised
2003	Mayrig (authentic Armenian Mediterranean cuisine)	Mayrig offers the warmth and welcoming experience of a grandmother's house. Mayrig is a fine dining experience that captures the history, tradition and subtle, authentic flavours. Mayrig's flagship sails nowadays from Beirut to Riyadh, Maldives, Yerevan and Cairo.
2004	Central kitchen	Centralised operations for catering and restaurants
2008	Fig holding franchises	The company is created for franchising opportunities, creation of manuals and legal work

Table 5.1. *(Continued)*

Established	Name of the Business	Service or Product Summarised
2011	'Mayrig Gourmet'	Offers pre-cooked frozen meals and original Armenian handcraft and gifts.
2013	Batchig (modern Armenian Lebanese cuisine)	Batchig's menu offers an array of Armenian Lebanese specialities, creating a new buzz of Armenian Mezze worldwide. Batchig is a garden, Batchig is a Shisha chill-out location. Batchig redefines live Armenian and Lebanese cooking at a whole new level.
2016	Mayrig Riyadh	Mayrig opens its doors in Riyadh, KSA
2017	Mayrig Yerevan	Mayrig opens its doors in Yerevan, Armenia
2018	Maldives consultancy	Promotes Mayrig's menu in the Maldives' Four Seasons Resort and Armenian food in general.
2021	Lahmajun (Armenian pizza)	Lahmajun is just another round, thin piece of dough topped with minced meat, vegetables and herbs. Lahmajun celebrates the Armenian culinary heritage through a trendy dish in all Middle Eastern cultures. (…) Lahmajun is a concept that can be bound in a location or incorporated in a food truck.
2022	Kamakian	A retail brand selling high-quality Armenian products made by Armenian and Lebanese mothers. Kamakian engages with its products, and over 400 farmers around Lebanon. Products are sold in stores in Lebanon, Dubai and the Maldives.
2022	Mayrig Cairo	Mayrig opens its doors in Cairo, Egypt
2022	Sandwichian	Healthy street food based on Silk Road spices for exotic flavours, serving soujouk sliders featuring Silk Road spices, cured meats,

(Continued)

Table 5.1. *(Continued)*

Established	Name of the Business	Service or Product Summarised
		yoghurt sauces, silky hummus and homemade pickles.
2023	Batchig city centre	Batchig opens its doors in the city centre of Beirut, Lebanon
2023	Batchig Sur Mer	Batchig opens its doors in Zaitunay Bay, Lebanon
2024	Batchig Bayada	Batchig opens its doors in Bayada, Lebanon

Source: Authors' creation.

Fig Holding's flagship brand is Mayrig, a restaurant established in 2003 in Beirut, Lebanon, the first avant-garde Armenian restaurant in the Middle East. Later, the company set up a catering service unit in 2004. Fig Holding includes the Central Kitchen which was established in 2004. In 2011, 'Mayrig Gourmet' opens as a destination for Armenian pre-cooked frozen meals, original handcraft and gifts. In 2013, in Beirut, a fast-casual hospitality concept was established called 'Batchig' (which translates from Armenian as a kiss), which operates as a fast-casual restaurant. After gaining recognition, Mayrig soon developed a franchising programme, which was first tested with franchised outlets established in Dubai (UAE) (2013) and Riyadh (KSA) (2016). In 2017, a third franchise restaurant was opened in Armenia's capital, Yerevan, which brought the Mayrig concept closer to its Armenian home country.

Further, the company established Maldives Consultancy to promote Mayrig's menu in the Four Seasons Resort in 2018. The business expanded into opening an Armenian breakfast and lunch fast food chain called Lahmajun, with 14 branches in Beirut, Geneva and Dubai. A retail line called Kamakian was founded in 2022, which promotes and sells high-quality homemade Armenian and Lebanese products produced by more than 400 farmers in Lebanon. The co-founder, Aline, also runs a YouTube channel, *Cook with Aline*. The latest addition of Fig Holding is Sandwichian, created in 2022.

Mission and Values

For Fig Holding's employees, who work in the hospitality business, respect for everyone is central. Everyone is respected and welcomed, regardless of nationality, religion, sexual orientation or social standing. Fig Holding's mission is 'We are passionate trendsetters who celebrate Armenian heritage through food and hospitality'. The company creates and implements culinary projects related to its Armenian heritage, whether from Mediterranean and Anatolian roots or in its globalised and urban inspirations of the Armenian diaspora.

Fig Holding's Values

Quality: We take pride in providing value-added products and services that ensure consistency and growth.

Belonging: We are committed to making Fig Holding a welcoming environment that promotes engagement, trust and growth to all our talent.

Innovation: Innovation is at the core of what we do. We use our creativity to set trends and lead the market.

Responsibility: We are an integral part of the communities in which we operate. We believe in providing care to our people and giving back to the environment and society.

Diversity: It is the catalyst of our success. We create an inclusive environment that promotes respect and equal chances of growth on all levels.

Company Background

The story of the Kamakian family business started in 2003 with the establishment of Mayrig, the first high-end authentic Armenian restaurant in the Arab world. The restaurant was founded by Aline Kamakian and her cousin, Serge and was later integrated into Fig Holding (see Table 5.1). The initial motivation to found Mayrig came from Aline, who wanted to 'realise' her late father's dream of opening an Armenian restaurant. Aline was passionate about cooking, and Mayrig, which means 'little mother' in Armenian, was meant to revive the forgotten flavours of Armenia, the homeland of the Kamakian family who fled the Ottoman Empire's genocide against Armenians in 1915 and were displaced in Lebanon.

Armenian food was mainly known as fast or street food in Lebanon, where people appreciate plates like Lahmajoun (Armenian Pizza), 'Soujouk' (sausages) and 'Basterma' (highly seasoned cured meat), which were sold in Bourj Hammoud, a vibrant Armenian neighbourhood in Beirut. Thousands of displaced Armenian refugees who had fled the genocide against the people in Turkey in the 1920s and later those who fled the annexation of the lands by Turkey (in 1939) had established themselves in Lebanon. Armenians had integrated into the country and built productive communities, contributing to the economy and society. The historical experiences of Armenians in Lebanon, characterised by past sufferings and loss and shared experiences of poverty during their early years of displacement, have marked the Armenian spirit and mindset (Rebeiz, 2023). Their experienced hardships have created a shared narrative among the Armenian community that focuses on empathy, generosity and community support, which has also been very present in the Kamakian family. The Armenians brought a rich food tradition, but their cuisine's diversity was less well-known. The family business wanted to transmit and share Armenian culture by creating the first high-end restaurant in Lebanon and the Middle East. It was also a way to give back to the (Armenian) society too.

Aline Kamakian, a passionate food chef, saw an opportunity to offer a vast array of healthy and traditional dishes and thus introduce the Lebanese people to the forgotten flavours of Armenia. Using recipes she learnt from her mother and grandmother, she established the Mayrig restaurant (see Fig. 5.1) which

Fig. 5.1.   Mayrig Restaurant. *Source:* Kamakian (n.d.).

introduced customers to unexplored dishes, such as 'Mante' (meat dumplings), Mayrig's signature dishes, 'Sou Beureg' and 'Wild Cherry Kebab.' Mayrig, located in a hip and central quarter of Beirut called Gemmayze, sometimes also called the Soho of Beirut, was an old quarter of Beirut with French townhouses and mandate architecture right next to Beirut port. Gemmayze offered a buzzing nightlife with bars, coffee shops, conceptual restaurants, clubs and art galleries.

The restaurant welcomes guests in a cosy, elegant ambience that recalls traditional Armenia.

Originally, the business was run as a partnership with Aline and her cousin; however, this partnership ended in 2019. Supported by her family, Aline bought out her cousin's share. Over the years, she has had a remarkable entrepreneurial career characterised by philanthropic leadership, inspiring others to make a positive impact. This is reflected in the company's culture and its care for its employees. For example, Fig Holding provides shares to employees dedicated to the business. As a result, more than 90% of them have stayed with the business. Today, Fig Holding is a growing family-to-corporate business run by the board of Fig Holding. The business employs more than 120 people in Lebanon and abroad. Fig Holding has made itself a name in the hospitality sector within the region and abroad. However, the business has faced numerous substantial challenges and threats to its existence, being based in Lebanon, one of the world's most volatile and politically risky countries.

During the COVID-19 pandemic, Lebanon was in a total lockdown, requiring Fig Holding to find alternatives to deliver food to people's homes. The business continues to operate the 'Lahmajun' food delivery brand to retain and keep employees in their jobs. 'Lahmajun' is originally a form of Armenian or Middle Eastern pizza with a 'quick bite in between' (see Fig. 5.2). It is a round, thin, slightly crispy dough topped with meat and spices, which is very popular in the region. 'Lahmajun', the business, moved from being a delivery solution to being rolled out in various locations in Beirut, and the brand has been sold in 10 different kitchens across Dubai since 2021. During the 2021 Expo in Dubai, the family business engaged with the street food concept and introduced 'Sandwichian', served from a food truck and offered 'silk road' fast food.

Fig Holding provided support and help to thousands of impoverished and diminished families who have suffered the consequences of Lebanon's economic crisis and also in the aftermath of the Beirut Port explosion in August 2020. Fig Holding added a social entrepreneurial venture to the company portfolio – 'Kamakian' – which works with over 400 Lebanese farmers in 2021. The company sells natural products, such as Armenian specialities, salts, jams and preserves, sauces and home-grown honey produced by women farmers from different parts of the country, e.g. the Beqaa Valley, Jbaa in the South, from the central Metn region and the northern shores of Anfeh. Kamakian sells its products in Lebanon and online to the vast Lebanese diaspora market, estimated to have 16 million Lebanese abroad (compared with less than four million in Lebanon) (Verdeil & Dewailly, 2019). Kamakian works mainly with women farmers and produces speciality products based on local resources and agricultural production. 'Kamakian' is Fig Holding's way of giving back to the land and the most vulnerable among its population. It is also a tribute to Lebanon, the country that welcomed thousands of Armenian refugees after they were expelled from their homeland and left with nothing.

Fig. 5.2.   Lahmajun. *Source:* Kamakian (n.d.).

SDG#1 Poverty Reduction at Fig Holding

In Lebanon, the home country of Fig Holding, the poverty levels have doubled, and health deprivation have tripled since 2019 (UNESCWA, 2023). The country has had very weak or non-existent social protection in the past, and people had very limited to no access to good public services, such as health and social aid, which disproportionally negatively affects vulnerable and poor populations. However, since the Fall of 2019, the country has been confronted with several consecutive massive crises:

- In addition to the COVID-19 pandemic, the country has suffered from one of the most severest economic crises in history;
- In 2019, Lebanon defaulted on its massive public debt (around $90 billion or 170% of GDP), leading to a currency crisis where the Lebanese pound lost over

95% of its value against the US dollar on the black market (World Bank Group, 2024);
- The crisis furthermore crippled Lebanon's banking sector, which imposed strict capital controls, locking depositors out of their US dollar accounts and savings.

In this context, Lebanese depositors have lost over $50–70 billion in savings trapped in the insolvent banking system (LCPS, 2020). In addition, Lebanon had to endure the Beirut Port explosion in August 2020. The port explosion was one of the largest non-nuclear explosions in recent history, and it had wide-ranging consequences for the Lebanese society and economy (CARE, 2021). The explosion caused an estimated $4.6 billion in physical damages (CARE, 2021). Schools, healthcare facilities, hospitals, living quarters and numerous businesses were destroyed, leading to economic losses between $2.9 and $3.5 billion (CARE, 2021; Nassar & Nastacă, 2021). More than 200 individuals lost their lives in the explosion, 6,500 were injured, and more than 300,000 people were displaced because their homes had been damaged or destroyed (Nassar & Nastacă, 2021). The explosion also destroyed Lebanon's only grain silos and different warehouses where food was stored for the country, which reduced the capacity to import and store cereals to 1/5 less of pre-explosion levels and disrupted the food supply of the country. Consequently, food prices soared 11 times the pre-crisis level and imposed food insecurity on 46% of Lebanese citizens and 50% of Syrian refugees in Lebanon. In Lebanon, the middle class has been shrinking to non-existence, and many people have fallen under the poverty line (Asi, 2022).

Beirut Port Explosion 2020 and the Aftermath

The Beirut Port explosion took place on August 4, 2020. The explosion's epicentre was just a few hundred metres away from Fig Holding's offices and the Mayrig restaurant, which were located in Gemmayzeh, separated from the explosion site only by a highway (Abou-Haka, 2023). It was still amid the COVID-19 pandemic, and the government had announced another lockdown from August 6th to 10th to curb the spread amidst a spike in cases. The Mayrig restaurant was open for only a few days to provide income for its employees. All staff members were present since they had few opportunities to work during the previous lockdown periods and needed to support families at home. Fig Holding held a management team meeting to discuss further strategies for the looming lockdown on the day of the explosion. The office was on the third floor overlooking the neighbourhood where they observed the firefighters trying to contain the flames in the port's grain silos. They even filmed the scene to share it on social media when the explosion went off and engulfed people, buildings, roads and everything. The immediate aftermath for Fig Holding and the Mayrig restaurant was dire: seven employees became irreversibly disabled on that very day, and 29 had to be hospitalised with bone fractures, cuts and other traumas; the offices, as well as the restaurant, were destroyed. Very few of the team members were still capable of functioning. Gemmayzeh, where Mayrig was located, had been destroyed; many people died there, and entire houses had collapsed or became uninhabitable. The Mayrig restaurant, the kitchen, the holding office and assets such as delivery cars were destroyed; the nearby family home was also destroyed. According to Aline, the business '*was minus zero*'. The board decided on the same day to return to work and rebuild everything. The next day, employees who could still help started cleaning up the area around the restaurant and Mayrig's destruction site. Aline visited all her 29 staff members in the hospital to reassure them that things would move on and Fig Holding was committed to taking care of their hospital costs.

Moreover, Fig Holding supported employees who had lost their homes because of the explosion, where they leveraged their social capital and contacted influential and wealthy people in their network who provided food and groceries, plates, fuel and other things. Donors were reluctant to give money then and focused more on material assistance. It became evident that Fig Holding needed to rebuild Mayrig and reopen the business as soon as possible so that the business would provide income and cash for its employees. A small contractor was convinced to rebuild the restaurant to a functional level within a week. The business used a crowdfunding campaign and pitched to several non-governmental organisations (NGOs) in Beirut to alleviate the situation. In this way, Fig Holding could raise financial resources from NGOs specialised in supporting businesses with their repairs. It also benefited from the solid and trustful relationships created since the beginning of Mayrig in 2003. Suppliers trusted and supplied the business with the necessary materials and resources to rebuild the company 'on credit' – Fig Holding would repay them slowly over the years. Fig Holding's actions fit SDG#1.5, which helps build the resilience of those in vulnerable situations and reduces their exposure and vulnerability to economic, social and environmental shocks and disasters. Aline summarises, 'And this is how we started again. So there were different levels. First of all, it was your attitude, devotion, stubbornness, and craziness that gave trust; that gave hope for others to do that.' (A. Kamakian, personal communication, March 2, 2024). It took nine months to rebuild Mayrig and about seven months to repair or rebuild the houses of Fig Holding employees or people indirectly connected with Fig Holding (for example, contractors, some suppliers, etc.). Altogether, Fig Holding supported 120 individuals and their families, showing alignment to SDG#1.4 by ensuring their employees who are poor and the vulnerable after the disaster have equal rights to economic resources, access to basic services and control of a safe shelter.

Rebuilding the Community

In the days after the blast, at Mayrig, there was no water or bread to eat, but the chef of the Batchig restaurant, which was on the eastern outskirts of Beirut that was unaffected by the explosion, brought sandwiches for the team. Aline realised that many other people were hungry in the vicinity, so she asked the Batchig chef to bring double the amount the next day. On the third day, Batchig delivered 300 sandwiches that were distributed to whoever asked for them. The team soon realised that people could not survive on sandwiches alone and began to cook from whatever they had. They cooked on open fires that consumed broken wood from the destroyed Mayrig restaurant and distributed food to whoever came. The business created makeshift tents with restaurant remnants for employees and families with nowhere to go by feeding people experiencing poverty, supporting SDG#1.1. What started with a temporary kitchen to provide providential meals for those in need turned into a full-fledged humanitarian action that provided 2,500–3,000 meals twice a day for several months. Fig Holding demonstrates their abilities to mobilise resources to implement initiatives that help to eradicate poverty, aligned with Target 1.a of SDG#1. Fig Holding teamed up with 'World Central Kitchen', an NGO that was founded in 2010 and that provides food relief in response to humanitarian, climate, and community crises. A year after the deadly explosion, the Mayrig team was still feeding 500 impoverished people a day whilst running the restaurant. World Central Kitchen supported the Fig Holding/Mayrig team and created the cooking infrastructure to supply meals on that scale daily; the NGO also provided a good part of the money necessary to buy the ingredients for each meal. Fig Holding's efforts aligned with indicator 1.4.1 in SDG#1 to ensure everyone can access basic needs such as food.

Fig Holding also leveraged their networks to provide financial aid for this initiative, which worked out because of the good personal reputation in the community. During the first weeks, people would come to Mayrig and receive their food boxes; later, however, the food distribution was coordinated by different NGOs, which would provide lists of eligible beneficiaries. Aline recalls,

> We worked with different NGOs because it's not my job (to logistically organise a full-fledged humanitarian program). I don't know how to do this. The NGOs used to tell me we need "this much and that much" and I used to do that and distribute what was requested. (A. Kamakian, personal communication, March 2, 2024)

The business had learnt a lot through this time and acquired several new capabilities necessary to be a good humanitarian agent. The business had to develop a different mindset, moving from an entrepreneurial mindset to solving problems and receiving help as a business and humanitarian. The team also learnt about the logistics of providing a community kitchen for needy people. Notably, they had to understand how to ensure food safety and storage, especially when handling perishable food with a flawed electricity supply under adverse conditions. Fig Holding learnt about community outreach and donor management and had to manage the collaboration with different NGOs efficiently. They contributed significantly to building the resilience of people experiencing poverty and those in vulnerable situations and reducing their exposure and vulnerability, as stated in SDG#1.5.

Engagement for Nagorno Karabach

In 2023, members of the Fig Holding team were called again to help tens of thousands of displaced and hungry people who had fled ethnic cleansing in

Berg-Karabach amid war and violence. There had been a long ongoing conflict between Armenia and Azerbaijan over the disputed Nagorno-Karabakh territory, which has an overwhelming ethnic Armenian population despite being internationally recognised as part of Azerbaijan. After a 44-day war in 2020 between both countries and a blockage of the area by Azerbaijan in December 2022, the conflict culminated in a comprehensive military assault dubbed an 'anti-terrorist operation' targeting the Armenian population. In October 2023, Azerbaijani forces gained control over Nagorno-Karabakh, leading to a mass exodus where the majority of the estimated 120,000 ethnic Armenians evacuated the region to Armenia (Sargsyan, 2024). Aline and her family, being also ethnic Armenians, had watched the news about this tragedy unfold and were reminded of the historic sufferance of their people. Hence, they immediately prepared to engage again. Fig Holding contacted World Central Kitchen, and they agreed to deploy a team to Armenia. Previous experiences working with World Central Kitchen on the frontlines of humanitarian disaster relief after the Beirut explosion taught the business the necessary skills to deal with massive food insecurity and impoverished populations. Within days, the Mayrig team was actionable by aligning themselves with contributing to SDG#1.3 to implement appropriate social protection systems and measures for the poor and vulnerable. Fig Holding convinced the management of the Mayrig franchisee in Armenia and several restaurant owners in Yerevan to participate in the initiatives, allowing them to provide over 1,200 meals a day. They also raised funds through different donors, which support Target 1.b of SDG#1 to back accelerated investment in poverty eradication actions and SDG#1.4, ensuring equal access to resources and basic services.

Aline remembers some of the challenges:

> We had a lot of malnutrition cases. We spoke with the doctors because people had suffered more than months of blockage before they escaped; most were suffering from malnutrition, and they couldn't digest the food we had prepared. So, we had to revert to less bloating food.

Spreading dignity and compassion combined with a warm meal made a difference for many and the business. It was also a sign of hope for these displaced people, which would support their physical and moral strength to continue with their lives. Their work illustrates an excellent example of target 1.a in SDG#1, where significant resources were mobilised through different sources and cooperation to support the basic needs of the displaced groups.

Further Engagement in Lebanon

Since October 2023, there has been an escalation of hostilities along the Lebanon-Israel border between Israel and Hezbollah. This armed militia has created an active conflict zone in the southern border areas of Lebanon and internally displaced more than 80,000 people (United Nations Office for the

Coordination of Humanitarian Affairs, 2024). Again, Fig Holding and Mayrig engaged and supplied meals for hundreds of people, aligning with Target 1.a of SDG#1 by mobilising resources to provide adequate and predictable means to reduce poverty. Yet, they limit their support to initially a few days or a week, and then people must be able to organise themselves alone, supporting SDG#1.4 to provide basic needs. For Aline, it is vital not to turn people into beggars and get them used to begging and depending on help, as she notices many people change from barely asking for help to becoming beggars. The decision is consistent with Target 1.2 of SDG#1, which aims to reduce poverty by providing opportunities to work with them. This is in the philosophy of Fig Holding: 'We receive so many beggars in front of Mayrig. They throw their head to the back (Lebanese gesture for "no") "as soon as we tell them", "Start to work with us". They're not interested. So, it's very important for us to get this; we believe there is work for everyone who wants to work' (A. Kamakian, personal communication, March 2, 2024). The business helps, but the principle is to provide help so that people can help themselves become independent and build a stronger future.

What Next for Fig Holding?

Despite not being a social venture, providing help to alleviate poverty and hunger has been an essential element of the business community engagement and culture, which shows alignment with SDG#1. As a result of the Beirut explosion, Fig Holding and members of the World Central Kitchen created Sawablessed ('together blessed') to continuously support displaced and impoverished people in Lebanon. Sawablessed also involved other members of the Beiruti food scene, such as Kamel Mouzawak, a leading advocate for supporting local farmers and the founder of Lebanon's first farmers' market. Sawablessed became an intrinsic part of Fig Holding's brands, allowing the company to keep raising money from different sources and donors and communicate transparently via social media about continuous activities to support the poor and needy. This initiative helps contribute to SDG#1.3, 1.4 and 1.5 to eradicate poverty in crises-laded countries like Lebanon.

For Fig Holding, it has been clear that business success is not just profit-making. It has significant responsibilities towards its employees and communities. Their restaurants have always paid as much attention to local sourcing as possible. Particularly with their lines of business, such as the Kamakian brand and their reliance on local agriculture, the business provides critical market access to women farmers, strengthening their livelihood and increasing women's income in rural communities, aligning with target 1.4 of SDG#1. It is a fundamental commitment of Fig Holding to invest in all-natural products sourced from farms with sustainable farming practices, which ultimately benefits local communities. The business has a long-term sustainability perspective. This philosophy is also reflected in how Fig Holding has dealt with its employees: supporting their employees by rebuilding their houses and apartments and paying for their hospital bills, which is not required by any law. Operating the business under adverse conditions allows them to keep employees and their families afloat, thus providing hope for the future and the assurance that their employer cares about them. While Lebanon struggles to emerge from crises, Fig Holding is determined to rebuild and rebound its communities and country with continuous efforts for sustainable development.

References

Abou-Haka, Y. (2023). Aline Kamakian: The rage to rebuild Mayrig. *L'orient Today*. https://today.lorientlejour.com/article/1345449/aline-kamakian-the-rage-to-rebuild-mayrig.html

Alvaredo, F., Assouad, L., & Piketty, T. (2021). *Measuring inequality in the Middle East*. In H. Hakimian (Ed.), *The Routledge handbook on the Middle East economy* (pp. 206–225). Routledge.

Asi, Y. (2022). Lebanon struggles to pick up the pieces after the beirut port explosion. *Arab Centre Washington DC*. https://arabcenterdc.org/resource/lebanon-struggles-to-pick-up-the-pieces-after-the-beirut-port-explosion/

CARE. (2021). 6 months later, Beirut blast still sends shock waves through Lebanese communities. https://www.care.org/news-and-stories/press-releases/6-months-later-beirut-blast-still-sends-shock-waves-through-lebanese-communities/

Kamakian, A. (n.d.). Aline Kamakian – Culinary Experience. *Aline Kamakian*.https://www.alinekamakian.com/our-impact

Khoury, R. (2019). How poverty and inequality are devastating the Middle East. *Carnegie Corporation of New York*. https://www.carnegie.org/our-work/article/why-mass-poverty-so-dangerous-middle-east/

LCPS. (2020). Lebanon's financial crisis: Where did the money go? old.lcps-lebanon.org/agendaArticle.php?id=158

Nassar, C. K., & Nastacă, C. C. (2021). The Beirut port explosion: Social, urban and economic impact. *Theoretical and Empirical Researches in Urban Management*, *16*(3), 42–52.

Rebeiz, M. (2023). The Israel-Lebanon maritime border agreement: Does Lebanon implicitly recognise the state of Israel? *Dickinson Law Review*, *128*(1), 197–231.

Sargsyan, T. (2024). The Aliyev regime's role in the ethnic cleansing of Nagorno-Karabakh Armenians. *Human Rights Foundation*. https://hrf.org/the-aliyev-regimes-role-in-the-ethnic-cleansing-of-nagorno-karabakh-armenians/

United Nations Economic and Social Commission for Western Asia (UNESCWA). (2023). *Second Arab multidimensional poverty report*. https://www.unescwa.org/publications/second-arab-multidimensional-poverty-report

United Nations Office for the Coordination of Humanitarian Affairs (OCHA). (2024). Lebanon: Flash Update #6-Escalation of hostilities in south Lebanon as of December 21 2023. https://www.unocha.org/publications/report/lebanon/lebanon-flash-update-6-escalation-hostilities-south-lebanon-21-december-2023

Verdeil, E., & Dewailly, B. (2019). International migration and the Lebanese diaspora. In E. Verdeil, G. Faour, & M. Hamzé (Eds.), *Atlas of Lebanon: New challenges* (pp. 42–43). Presses de l'IFPO.

World Bank Group. (2024). The World Bank in Lebanon. https://www.worldbank.org/en/country/lebanon/overview

Chapter 6

India: From Poverty to Decent Living – A Case of Pune, India

Aditi Mishra and Niharika Singh

Symbiosis International (Deemed) University, India

Introduction

Poverty is a multifaceted issue that manifests differently across the globe, affecting various populations with distinct challenges and requiring tailored efforts for its elimination. The United Nations Development Programme (UNDP) has established 17 Sustainable Development Goals (SDGs) to address a wide range of socio-economic issues, emphasising the need for interconnected actions across different sectors (UNDP, 2020). Specifically, SDG#1 focuses on eradicating poverty, targeting the most vulnerable populations by improving access to essential resources and services.

Family members organisations, whether reputable over generations or freshly established, have an extensive effect on financial and social growth. They play an important function in eliminating destitution in India by offering work, boosting well-being and promoting the ability to grow, therefore resolving essential stimulants of destitution. India flaunts a lengthy background of family member services businesses, such as Tata, Godrej and Reliance, coupled with Kirloskar, which have added considerably to employment figures. In addition, the business social responsibility (CSR) campaigns taken on by these family members organisations play a crucial responsibility in dealing with destitution within the system.

The chapter provides insights into the above by exploring the case of a small family business in Pune, Maharashtra, India. Despite its modest size, this firm was selected for its significant contribution to entrepreneurial activities and its transformative impact on the lives of its employees. The business, named 'Naani's Litti Chokha' was established in 2020 by Mr. Abhishek Kumar, a former Sales Manager who left his job during the COVID-19 pandemic due to health concerns and decided to venture into entrepreneurship. Naani's Litti Chokha is a family-owned restaurant enterprise founded by Mr. Abhishek Kumar, a first-generation entrepreneur. The establishment has set a dual objective aimed at combating absolute poverty. First, it seeks to offer nutritious food at affordable

Attaining the 2030 Sustainable Development Goal of No Poverty, 69–81
Copyright © 2025 Aditi Mishra and Niharika Singh
Published under exclusive licence by Emerald Publishing Limited
doi:10.1108/978-1-83608-570-620241006

prices. Second, it endeavours to create employment opportunities for unskilled daily wage workers. This socially driven business model has earned Naani's Litti Chokha significant acclaim within a relatively brief period.

Vision and Mission Statement for Naani's Litti Chokha

Vision

To be a leading force in eradicating poverty by transforming the dining experience into a catalyst for social change, where every meal contributes to a healthier, more equitable society.

Mission

- Nourishing Communities: To provide delicious and nutritious food at affordable prices, ensuring access to healthy meals for all.
- Empowering Individuals: To create meaningful employment opportunities for unskilled daily wage workers, fostering their development and improving their quality of life through stable jobs and skills training.
- Sustainable Growth: To grow our business sustainably, prioritising the well-being of our employees and customers while positively impacting the wider community.
- Cultural Preservation: To celebrate and promote the rich culinary heritage of our region, offering authentic dishes that bring people together and preserve traditional flavours.

By adhering to these principles, Naani's Litti Chokha aims to be more than just a restaurant; it strives to be a pillar of community support and a beacon of hope in the fight against poverty.

Products Offered by Naani's Litti Chokha

Naani's Litti Chokha has garnered considerable acclaim for its signature dish, Litti Chokha, a traditional culinary delicacy from Bihar, India. The founder, Mr. Abhishek Kumar, originally from Bihar, initiated this business with the goal of providing healthy, affordable food to the community. Initially, the restaurant's offerings resonated primarily with the native Bihari population. However, as the health benefits of the cuisine became widely recognised, the customer base expanded to include individuals from diverse regions. The restaurant's menu has grown to include a variety of dishes, such as Litti Chicken, Sattu Paratha, Vegetarian Thali, Poori and Mutton Curry (Fig. 6.1).

This expansion reflects the increasing popularity and demand for Naani's Litti Chokha's nutritious and reasonably priced meals, contributing to the business's steady growth and wider appeal. Nani's Litti Chokha attracts patrons from diverse socio-economic backgrounds. While the Mutton Curry is particularly

Fig. 6.1. Naani's Litti Chokha Menu.

favoured by individuals from higher socio-economic classes, dishes such as the Vegetarian Thali, Litti Chokha and Litti Chicken enjoy widespread popularity across all classes. These latter offerings have become staples for a broad demographic, reflecting the restaurant's commitment to providing inclusive, nutritious meals that appeal universally.

Background of Naani's Litti Chokha

Abhishek's interest in food and cooking nurtured during his early childhood while living with his maternal grandparents, who played a pivotal role in his business endeavour. He attributes his culinary passion and subsequent business success to his maternal grandmother ('nani'), in whose honour the business is named. Originally from Bihar, Abhishek migrated to Pune 15 years ago in search of employment and initially worked as a salesperson for a pharmaceutical company. Over a decade, he advanced to the position of Regional Manager and was performing well in his career. However, the pandemic in 2020 posed significant health risks for those in the pharmaceutical industry, prompting Abhishek to pursue his long-standing interest in food by opening his restaurant on December 25, 2020.

This venture received robust support from his parents, particularly his father, Mr. Dinanath Singh, who decided to invest and become a partner in the business. Mr. Singh, originally a farmer, collaborated with his son to establish this first-generation family enterprise, thus marking the inception of Naani's Litti Chokha. The initial setup of 'Naani's Litti Chokha' included a single employee who had migrated from Bihar to work as a construction labourer under third-party supervision, earning daily wages. Mr. Abhishek Kumar is currently training his sister to assume the managerial role at Naani's Litti Chokha. This initiative aims to ensure effective business management and continuity, reflecting a strategic approach to leadership development within the family-owned enterprise. By 2024, the business expanded its workforce to five employees, demonstrating its growing popularity among customers and its employees' enhanced standard of living. This case study highlights the potential of small family businesses to drive entrepreneurial growth and improve socio-economic conditions, thereby contributing to poverty alleviation. Naani's Litti Chokha is registered on prominent online food ordering platforms Swiggy and Zomato. The restaurant consistently receives positive customer feedback, maintaining an average rating of over four out of five stars. This high level of customer satisfaction underscores the quality and appeal of the restaurant's offerings.

 ˗ Established on December 25, 2020, this family-owned restaurant has experienced substantial growth over the past three years. Mr. Abhishek Kumar aged 41, a first-generation businessperson and former Sales Manager, has cultivated strong relationships with his customers. Starting with a single staff member in a 100-square-foot space, the restaurant has expanded to 700 square feet today, accommodating a fully operational restaurant along with living quarters for staff. Mr. Kumar prioritises the well-being of his staff, ensuring they have access to quality meals three times daily at the restaurant. He has also extended this provision to include their families, alleviating their concerns about providing meals while working full-time. This policy has significantly enhanced employee retention, as food and accommodation are fully covered by Mr. Abhishek.

Specialising in authentic Bihari cuisine, a hallmark of Mr. Abhishek's hometown, the restaurant has established a unique selling proposition that has garnered significant popularity. To maintain the authenticity and quality of this cuisine, Abhishek exclusively hires staff from Bihar who possesses knowledge of Bihari flavours and culinary traditions.

From the outset of his business, Mr. Abhishek pledged to empower women and unskilled workers from lower socio-economic backgrounds, aiming to improve their circumstances. Given Bihar's high levels of unemployment and poverty, he sees his restaurant as a vehicle for contributing positively to his home state. By hiring individuals from the lower, unskilled, daily wage-earning segment of society and providing them with training opportunities within his restaurant, Mr. Abhishek believes he is making a meaningful social and economic impact and contributing to SDG#1.1 – eradicate extreme poverty and SDG#1.2 – reduce poverty by at least 50%.

Key Milestones in the Naani's Litti Chokha Family Business

- December 2020: Establishment of Nani's Litti Chokha (Naani's Litti Chokha) in a 100-square-foot area, initially offering only Litti Chokha.
- March 2021: Temporary closure of the restaurant due to the peak of the COVID-19 pandemic.
- July 2021: Relocation of the restaurant to a 280-square-foot space in response to the second wave of COVID-19.
- January 2022: Expansion of the menu to include Litti Chicken and an increase in staff to two members.
- August 2022: Relocation to a 700-square-foot area and introducing Sattu Poori to the menu in response to the increase in customer base.
- September 2022: Expansion of staff to 5–6 members and further expansion of the menu to include vegetarian and non-vegetarian food.
- January 2023: Introduction of the Vegetarian Thali to the menu as an extremely affordable lunch option for lower and middle-class workers.
- February 2023: Opening of a new branch in a different location (Hinjewadi, Pune).
- January 2024: Introduction of catering services for small parties and get togethers at an affordable price.

These milestones highlight significant phases in the growth and adaptation of Naani's Litti Chokha, reflecting the business's resilience and expansion amid challenging circumstances, being dedicated to its commitment towards contribution to SDG#1.1 – eradicate extreme poverty and SDG#1.2 – reduce poverty by at least 50%.

Naani's Litti Chokha and SDG#1

In this section of the chapter, we have examined three key themes to understand the poverty alleviation measures aligned with SDG#1.1 – eradicating extreme poverty, SDG#1.3 Social Protection Systems and Measures and SDG#1.4 Equal Rights to Economic Resources. By so doing, we understand how this small family business is proactively engaging and playing a part in the fight against poverty, as well as improving the quality of life of its workforce.

First, examining the policy, which deals with the theme of Eradicating Extreme Poverty, we look at how the business provides opportunities and supports its employees to emerge from hardcore poverty. This involves the analysis of remunerations, amenities and other provisions for those with a new job and coming from a low-income background. The business ensures to maintain good quality food at affordable prices to ensure inclusivity of all income classes to meet its goal of poverty eradication.

Second, the analysis made on the theme of Social Protection Systems focuses on the business' respect of labour laws and the enforcement of quality health and safety measures and practices. This also includes examining matters of flexible working arrangements, parental and other forms of family leave and any other programs or activities that may enhance the physical and mental health, satisfaction and productivity of employees.

Third, Equal Rights to Economic Resources addresses the extent to which the business offers chances for staff upgrading and enhanced proficiency. This also entails evaluating the ongoing learning and participation programs, vocational and career training that enhance the ability of employees to advance their standard of living and protect their livelihoods in the event of job losses. Paying equal wages to male and female employees. This has empowered the female employees of Naani's Litti Chokha in finances through online payments and opening of bank accounts.

Naani's Litti Chokha and SDG#1.1 – Eradicating Extreme Poverty

Extreme poverty remains a significant concern in Maharashtra despite its status as one of India's economically advanced states. Historically, the state exhibited robust economic growth exceeding the national average during the 1980s but has since experienced a deceleration, now growing slightly below the national rate (Mishra & Panda, 2005).

The reduction in extreme poverty rates can be attributed primarily to increased employment opportunities stemming from entrepreneurial activities and a shift from traditional, low-wage occupations to more lucrative employment avenues. Participants of Naani's Litti Chokha in our study underscored the transformative impact of employment on their livelihoods. For instance, we heard from Ms. Kumari, a 28-year-old employee of Naani's Litti Chokha, how transitioning to a new job significantly boosted her monthly income from a mere 500 rupees to 12,000 rupees, despite her husband continuing in his previous labourer role (Ms. Kumari, personal communication, May 2024).

Similarly, another 28-year-old female employee also shared her experience of entering the workforce for the first time, joining her husband in Pune to improve their family's financial situation. Starting as a utensil cleaner, she now earns 9,000 rupees monthly, complemented by her husband's 15,000 rupees from his hotel job, collectively ensuring a sustainable living standard for their household. Moreover, Mr. Chaupal, aged 29, emphasised how securing a better paying position at Naani's Litti Chokha enabled him to enhance his income to 15,000 rupees per month, significantly improving his financial stability and enabling savings (Mr. Chaupal, personal communication, May 2024). Another employee at Naani's Litti Chokha, reported that since commencing employment, he facilitated the repayment of a 1.5 lakh loan within one year. This financial relief has enabled his family to emerge from extreme poverty, leading to an improved standard of living in their village while he earns a livelihood in Pune.

In addition to the contributions of its employees, the business is committed to offering healthy and nutritious food to lower income individuals at affordable prices, as evidenced by customer reviews. This initiative significantly benefits construction workers and other individuals from lower income brackets, providing them with access to daily sustenance at minimal cost.

These narratives underscore the critical role of employment in poverty alleviation by the family business within Pune and reflect broader trends in Maharashtra, where access to better paying jobs emerges as a pivotal factor in improving living standards and reducing economic vulnerability among marginalised populations.

Naani's Litti Chokha and SDG#1.3 Social Protection Systems and Measures

Decent living entails having access to the basic necessities of daily life. With changes in the employment sector, people can afford a decent living and move out of poverty. Family businesses that offer employment within their local communities help improve the standard of living and ensure access to daily needs as evidenced by the following statement from an employee at Naani's Litti Chokha:

> Since I started working at this place, my savings have increased. We managed to buy a small piece of land in our hometown, Darbhanga, Bihar, through a combination of savings and a bank loan. Additionally, my daily expenses have decreased because I receive all my meals at work, and my son gets one meal at the Anganwadi. (Naani's Litti Chokha employee, personal communication, May 2024)

Empowering women and providing decent living through employment, this restaurant has taken a significant initiative, as shared by another employee:

> Upon commencing employment, I acquired the financial means to address the needs of my children adequately. This included the ability to promptly seek medical attention in case of illness without the necessity of waiting for my husband's financial contribution. This employment has enabled me to save a small amount daily, providing a financial buffer for emergencies. My earnings are predominantly allocated to daily necessities such as vegetables, fruits, and snacks for my children. (Naani's Litti Chokha employee, personal communication, May 2024)

Enhancing the standard of living through home improvement and financial security is exemplified by another respondent's experience:

> Through my employment at this restaurant, I have saved enough
> money to reconstruct my kachha house into a pakka house in my
> native place. Additionally, I have opened a bank account to save
> for my daughter's education. These savings have increased my
> purchasing power, allowing me to meet basic needs better.
> (Naani's Litti Chokha employee, personal communication, May
> 2024)

Naani's Litti Chokha and SDG#1.4 Equal Rights to Economic Resources

Employment shifts also contribute to the enhancement of individual skills. In this
case study, we observe people transitioning from labour-intensive jobs to
restaurant work, requiring a different skill set. The restaurant has played a pivotal
role in rapidly enhancing the skills of its employees. This shift is illustrated by a
respondent's experience:

> Previously, I worked as a labourer, spending the entire day putting
> cement into the mixing machine. Now, I prepare vegetables and
> litti and maintain hygiene in the restaurant. Customer praise for
> the food we prepare boosts my morale and encourages me to learn
> more skills. (Ms. Kumari, personal communication, May 2024)

Transitioning from handling minor responsibilities to engaging in more skilled
tasks increases pay and benefits the restaurant by fostering peer collaboration and
learning, thereby creating a harmonious work environment. This is reflected in the
following examples of staff experiences: I began working as a utensil cleaner and
have since taken the initiative to prepare litti and vegetables. Additionally, I can
assume the responsibilities of others when they are on leave (Naani's Litti Chokha
employee, personal communication, May 2024).

> I initially joined as a kitchen helper, but I have since upgraded my
> skills to manage online orders and handle their dispatch through
> various methods. Additionally, I personally deliver nearby food
> orders. During peak work hours or festivals, I assist in food
> preparation and attend to customers' table orders. (Mr.
> Chaupal, personal communication, May 2024)

Another employee who commenced at Naani's Litti Chokha in May 2024 has
acquired proficiency in tasks such as vegetable chopping, cleaning and dough
preparation, skills previously unfamiliar to him but now integral to his role. These
competencies are expected to enhance his effectiveness and contribute to his
ongoing professional development at the establishment.

In the current competitive environment, achieving work–life balance is essential for rejuvenation. When asked which has been more beneficial – working here or previously as a labourer – Ms. Kumari responded:

> Both have equally benefited me. My earnings remain the same as before, but I now spend less on daily meals. I have a break in the afternoon, allowing me to pick up my son from school, feed him, and rest. After two hours, I return to work in the evening, bringing my son along so I can supervise him. We both have dinner at the restaurant before heading home to sleep. This arrangement allows me to spend time with my son while continuing to work. (Ms. Kumari, personal communication, May 2024)

An employee, who had never worked previously, indicated that she was initially apprehensive about working due to having four children and having concerns about balancing her time with them. However, the work arrangements at Naani's Litti Chokha accommodates a two-hour break for meals at the restaurant, and the leave policy is flexible. Residing near one's workplace contributes significantly to work–life balance and decreases overall expenditure, as highlighted by Mr. Chaupal: My accommodation, provided and covered by the employer, facilitates convenience in my work. Additionally, I benefit from a two-hour break during shifts. This accommodation allows me to reside with my family, which enables me to support my daughter's education (Mr. Chaupal, personal communication, May 2024).

Ensuring work–life balance also necessitates job security, as the pressure of job insecurity can impede one's ability to attend to family emergencies. This restaurant supports its employees in managing family emergencies by offering adequate holidays and resources. One employee said that she

> …. had to attend my sister's wedding in my hometown, and I took one month's leave in advance, returning to work at the same establishment afterwards. Additionally, I take two days off each month to address family matters such as banking and ration needs. (Naani's Litti Chokha employee, personal communication, May 2024)

The following table, Table 6.1, highlights the activities of Naani's Litti Chokha and more specifically shows how its activities are aligned with the targets of SGG#1.

Naani's Litti Chokha Stakeholders and SDG#1

The stakeholders at Naani's Litti Chokha are like those in other businesses, encompassing employees, customers, suppliers, the community and regulatory bodies. Their enduring support enables Naani's Litti Chokha to uphold its vision

Table 6.1. SDG#1 and Activities to Address the Goal.

Target No.	Targets	How Naani's Litti Chokha Addresses the Targets of SDG#1
1.1	By 2030, eradicate extreme poverty for all people everywhere, currently measured as people living on less than $1.25 a day (Indian Rupees 105 per day)	Naani's Litti Chokha addresses this objective by ensuring that employees receive an adequate monthly salary. When calculated on a daily basis, this remuneration amounts to 110 Indian Rupees per day, which exceeds the global poverty threshold. This minimum pay is guaranteed for all employees, thereby preventing them from experiencing financial hardship.
1.2	By 2030, reduce at least by half the proportion of men, women and children of all ages living in poverty in all its dimensions according to national definitions	Naani's Litti Chokha has a substantial proportion of female employees, in addition to male employees, thereby fostering increased female participation in the workforce. This dual employment within families, where both male and female members are working, significantly enhances the living standards of their children.
1.3	Implement nationally appropriate social protection systems and measures for all, including floors, and by 2030 achieve substantial coverage of the poor and the vulnerable	Naani's Litti Chokha prioritises the health and well-being of each employee. Salaries are disbursed directly into employees' individual bank accounts. The children of its employees attend government schools, where education is provided free of charge and mid-day meals are offered. Additionally, some employees have been able to upgrade their temporary (kachha) houses to permanent (pakka) houses through their savings and financial assistance

Table 6.1. *(Continued)*

Target No.	Targets	How Naani's Litti Chokha Addresses the Targets of SDG#1
		from banks. Employees are granted sufficient leave during medical emergencies and are supported in accessing superior medical facilities at nearby hospitals.
1.4	By 2030, ensure that all men and women, in particular the poor and the vulnerable, have equal rights to economic resources, as well as access to basic services, ownership and control over land and other forms of property, inheritance, natural resources, appropriate new technology and financial services, including microfinance	Naani's Litti Chokha addresses social protection at a micro-level, which positively impacts key socio-economic indicators. By facilitating land ownership in employees' native places, Naani's Litti Chokha promotes economic stability and asset building. Additionally, it nurtures a culture of savings and prudent utilisation of resources for children's education and health. The credibility established through their bank accounts enables employees to access small loans. As a result, male and female employees who were previously below the poverty line now experience an improved quality of life, benefiting from increased daily wages and a balanced work–life environment.
1.5	By 2030, build the resilience of the poor and those in vulnerable situations and reduce their exposure and vulnerability to climate-related extreme events and other economic, social and environmental shocks and disasters	Employees at Naani's Litti Chokha have developed significant resilience to vulnerabilities. This has been achieved through the provision of regular monthly income, access to nutritious food, adequate accommodation, and flexible working conditions.

and mission. Naani's Litti Chokha employees are well-acquainted with the working environment and perform their tasks diligently to ensure that the services provided meet customer satisfaction. Naani's Litti Chokha offers diverse training programs to its employees, enhancing their skills and knowledge in various areas. These programs include peer-to-peer teaching of new culinary techniques, training on health hygiene and childcare, and financial planning education. Such initiatives ensure that employees not only benefit from government schemes but also actively contribute to improving their lifestyles.

The community surrounding Naani's Litti Chokha has witnessed its growth and appreciates its presence, recognising Naani's Litti Chokha's efforts in supporting underprivileged communities and caring for local animals. During the COVID-19 pandemic, Naani's Litti Chokha further demonstrated its commitment by providing essential supplies and daily necessities to the nearby community.

Challenges of Working With SDG#1

India, a country rich in diverse cultures and customs, spans from north to south and east to west, presents a complex and fluctuating economy with ever-changing prices and market conditions. Businesses in India face intertwined challenges related to managing cultural diversity and economic environments. At Naani's Litti Chokha, these challenges are particularly evident. The continuous rise in raw material costs makes it difficult to maintain consistent food prices throughout the year, impacting Mr. Kumar's vision of providing affordable meals. During festival seasons, workforce availability decreases, and customer footfall slows down, disrupting capital flow and complicating the maintenance of employee pay scales.

Moreover, Mr. Kumar, and ostensibly Naani's Litti Chokha, face the challenge of maintaining operational efficiency amidst diverse cultural expectations and practices. The varied cultural norms across different regions necessitate tailored approaches to employee management, customer service and community engagement. Additionally, fluctuating economic conditions, such as inflation and market volatility, further complicate financial planning and stability. Mr. Kumar and Naani's Litti Chokha must also contend with regulatory changes and compliance requirements, which can vary significantly across states. Adapting to these regulations requires continuous monitoring and adjustments to operational procedures. The pressure to innovate and adopt new technologies while managing costs adds another layer of complexity.

In summary, Naani's Litti Chokha challenges are multifaceted, arising from the interplay of cultural diversity, economic fluctuations and regulatory demands. Addressing these challenges is crucial for Naani's Litti Chokha to maintain its vision of providing affordable and high-quality services to its stakeholders.

Conclusion

Family businesses represent a significant and diverse segment within the global economic landscape, making substantial contributions to economies worldwide. In India, these businesses have historically played a pivotal role in the national economy, contributing significantly to the gross domestic product (GDP). Whether longstanding entities with deep-rooted legacies or newly established ventures, family-owned enterprises exert profound influences on both economic and social development. They are instrumental in alleviating poverty in India by generating employment, enhancing overall well-being and fostering skill development, thereby addressing fundamental drivers of poverty.

This chapter delved into these dynamics by examining a small family business located in Pune, Maharashtra, India. Founded in 2020 by Mr. Abhishek Kumar, this restaurant employs five individuals and supports five households, as all employees and their families dine at the establishment. Through detailed discussions and in-depth interviews with employees, the study reveals significant improvements in work–life balance, living standards and skill development. Many employees have utilised their earnings to repay loans in their native villages, purchase land, build homes and contribute to siblings' weddings – all attributed to their employment at Naani's Litti Chokha restaurant.

Furthermore, the restaurant's policy of allowing women to bring their children to work and providing meals for them has facilitated continued female workforce participation without the constraints of early departure from work. These outcomes underscore the profound societal impacts family businesses can have by empowering women and lower income labourers, alleviating poverty, enhancing skills and promoting a dignified standard of living.

References

Mishra, S., & Panda, M. (2005). *Growth and poverty in Maharashtra.* Indira Gandhi Institue of Development Research. http://www.igidr.ac.in/pdf/publication/WP-2006-001.pdf

UNDP. (2020). *The SDGs in action.* United Nations Development Programme. https://www.undp.org/africa/waca/sdgs-action

Chapter 7

UAE: Food ATM – Addressing Poverty and Hunger Through Empathy

Jacinta Dsilva

SEE Institute, The Sustainable City, Dubai, UAE

Introduction

In the rapidly developing United Arab Emirates (UAE), an innovative initiative called the 'Food ATM' was launched in 2019 to tackle critical issues: poverty and hunger. This social enterprise aims to ensure that everyone, specifically the expatriate labour class in the UAE has access to nutritious food and respites their families back home from poverty. By combining empathy, technology and community involvement, Food ATM's initiative is reshaping how we think about food security and social responsibility.

Despite its wealth, the UAE faces challenges with economic inequality and food wastage. Beneath the modern skyscrapers and busy markets, there are still those who struggle with food insecurity and poverty. Recognising this, Ayesha Khan, an Indian expatriate from an IT and Telecommunication background, along with her husband Mr. Sajid Khan founded the social enterprise, Food ATM in 2019 in the UAE. Bearing witness to hunger and poverty as a teenager and experiencing it herself after losing her parents at the age of 16, she always felt empathetic towards those people who lived hand to mouth in a foreign country like the UAE. Food ATM is a registered entity in Ajman (one of the Emirate in the UAE) set up to provide low-cost food to blue-collar workers in the UAE. The idea behind Food ATM is simple yet impactful. This business not only addresses hunger but also promotes sustainable practices by reducing food waste and reducing poverty of the labour class.

Empathy is at the heart of the Food ATM initiative – understanding and addressing the needs of the less fortunate. This social enterprise demonstrates how a society can use its resources and technology to create a safety net for its most vulnerable members. By providing easy and dignified access to food, the initiative helps maintain the self-respect of those receiving assistance, avoiding the stigma often associated with traditional food aid eventually allowing the workers to send their maximum share back to their poor families.

Attaining the 2030 Sustainable Development Goal of No Poverty, 83–92
Copyright © 2025 Jacinta Dsilva
Published under exclusive licence by Emerald Publishing Limited
doi:10.1108/978-1-83608-570-620241007

This case study explores the beginnings, execution and impact of a social enterprise – Food ATM – in the UAE. It looks at the cooperative efforts of various stakeholders, especially the family, the challenges faced and the inspirational stories of individuals whose lives have been positively affected by this remarkable initiative embarked upon by Ayesha and her family members. Through this exploration, we aim to show how empathy-driven innovation can lead to a more inclusive and sustainable future. Increased productivity at the individual level leads to higher wages and improved job security, which directly reduces poverty. Enhanced skills and efficiency enable workers to generate more income, improving their living standards and access to education, healthcare and other essential services (OECD, 2018; World Bank, 2020). Food ATM offers nutritious meals at less than one dollar to individuals of any demographic, particularly blue-collar workers. These meals have allowed the workers to not only sustain and be productive but also to support their poor and debt-ridden families back home. With the help of additional money, the workers save, they can send back more share to their families, ultimately, removing their families from poverty and providing them with a reasonable standard of living. According to Gulf news (a popular newspaper in the UAE), low-income workers send 75–80% of their salaries back home. This money has allowed some of the worker families to stay alive, pay rent, send their children to school and overall have a better quality of life, thus, contributing to SDG#1.

Vision and Mission

SDG#1 is something all human beings must be involved in, it is not a global task, each of us is responsible for poverty, not succeeding. All of us together can solve this, Ayesha Khan the founder of Food ATM believes.

Therefore, Food ATM aims to tackle 'No Poverty' and 'Zero Hunger' SDGs by supporting the affordability of the meals, allowing workers and labourers to retain a higher portion of their salary to utilise it for better purposes such as offering good quality education to their children. Furthermore, the meals provide generous portions to ensure that every meal would keep the employees well-fed, contributing to their health and well-being.

Products and/or Services Offered by the Family Business

Food ATM provides meals to the lowest income individuals in the UAE for roughly three Arab Emirati Dirhams (AED), that is less than one dollar per meal. Everyone who avails the services of Food ATM has a card akin to that of a credit card and depending upon the payment made for an individual, the meal counts are added to the card for the entire month. The card is loaded at the start of every month. This card has a number, the individual's photo and a QR code on it, which is scanned for meal count balance. Individuals or companies sponsoring a worker must pay for the meals in advance. The card is accordingly loaded with meal counts. The card also carries the consumer's company ID and the company name with contact details. Roughly 10–12,000 hot meals are produced per day. Food ATM also runs a fully functioning National Food Lost and Waste Initiative in which left over or unwanted food from grocery stores are given to Food ATM rather than sending to the landfill to either be served with the hot meal or a bruised/bad fruit is sent to compost to be deposited in the soil, thus planting and nurturing more trees.

Background to the Family and the Business

The total population of UAE as of June 2024 is 10.24 million, where the local Emirati population stands at 11.48%, and the rest of the 88% of the population is expatriate of which 60% belong to low-income category or blue-collar workers (Global Media Insights, 2024). In the UAE, the poverty rate, which classifies individuals who earn less than 80 AED a day, is 19.5%, although this figure is not absolute due to lack of updated data. The poorest members of society in the UAE are usually blue-collar workers, cleaners and nannies who mostly come from South and Southeast Asia in search of better wages and salaries for themselves and their families back home. Some initiatives the UAE has facilitated include The Sheikh Khalifa Foundation which focuses on the health and education of citizens within the UAE and outside of the UAE. Another social assistance initiative is the Masaei Al Khair initiative that aims to provide low-income families with social security benefits (National Committee on the Sustainable Development Goals, n.d.).

On the other hand, for 12 years, Ayesha Khan was providing home-cooked meals for the cleaners, gardeners and drivers at her workplace in an IT engineering office in the UAE, at her own cost and her personal satisfaction, for roughly 15 or more people a month, allowing for those individuals to have 60 or more meals free per month. The impact was large although Ayesha did not understand just how extensive that impact was at first until she began engaging in lengthier and deeper conversations with the workers at her office that she understood that the lack of food worries allowed for more money to be sent back to the native countries of the workers where their loved ones could get the medical help they needed, rent could be paid and that their children were finally able to attend school. She decided to be proactive in providing good quality and nutritious food for the workers. Therefore, she started looking for protein-rich recipes on the internet that could be nutritious and help workers become more productive at their jobs and their families to come out of poverty. This impact led to Ayesha embarking on a journey to try and establish Food ATM in 2019 in Ajman (one of the Emirate in the UAE), but it was a struggle. She approached the Minister of Economic Development in an attempt to bring her idea of an economical food centre to light, but she was told that she needed fully functioning kitchens, health and safety checks, hygiene checks and staff that would number in the thousands, none of which she had.

Ayesha admitted that she nor her family members knew anything about the food industry or to do with the establishment of the food centre with regards to how the Minister of Economic Development rationalised it. She only knew that she had promised herself when she was young and hungry that one day, when she starts earning money, she will feed those whose pocket size is small. Ayesha mentioned, *if you are rich or poor, it has nothing to do with hunger, we both feel hungry equally and we should eat something when we are hungry.* She discussed the matter with her husband Mr. Sajid Khan, who was a bit apprehensive about the idea at first since they were just settling comfortably with two salaries and their children were able to go to a good school. However, the only thing Ayesha had in her mind was that she needed money, thus she decided to sell her land and other property in India to get at least AED one million to start this project. Ayesha's extended family thought she was insane and did not understand her vision for the enterprise until they saw her initiative on social media and other press getting recognised.

The first year of Food ATM was a 'complete failure', Ayesha said, since Food ATM had absolutely no business, people did not believe in the idea and other shops and cafeterias looked upon her with competitive derision. But things turned around in 2020, when the COVID-19 pandemic hit the entire world. She was asked to offer food to quarantine centres where people were isolated from their families and suffering from COVID-19. She started supplying food at the minimal price of AED 3 and her business began to expand. She started realising that cost inflation was a huge challenge, and it began impacting the business severely since with AED 3 per meal it was unable to sustain for a long time. Raw materials were extremely expensive due to short supply in the market; however, the meals had to be AED 3, as that was the brand identity of Food ATM. But suppliers were a saving grace since once they understood the purpose of the business they allowed for extensive overdrafts. As Ayesha put it, *the suppliers would not ask for that payment until I invited them to collect their dues.* She further mentioned that, *in a time when absolutely no one was meant to be venturing around, I had flexibility because I had a food permit for the labourers.*

Food ATM was able to rapidly grow to a place where it is currently able to provide 10–12,000 meals per five fully active kitchens and an 18% profit margin. The business also has a food exchange programme where people can give in food that is not 'pretty looking' and in return receive hot meals. Ayesha had also founded the National Food Lost and Waste Initiative to prevent food from going to landfill. An example she gave was that 90,000 kg of unused fruits from a grocery store was given to Food ATM rather than being sent to landfill. With this discarded food, 60% were used for giving to the needy and the 40% that were deemed 'bad' was sent off to compost and to then be deposited in the ground, which resulted in plants. Food ATM has also partnered with schools to have children visit their space; one of the favourite activities is when the children are working on the farm, located in Ras al Khadijah, and could produce fruits and vegetables. Food ATM currently works with municipalities, civil defence, economic development department and during the 2024 floods in UAE, Food ATM was the main operator in providing food services to all the people who were stranded in different locations.

As mentioned earlier, Mr. Sajid Khan, Ayesha's husband, was apprehensive about the idea and her family members back in India would initially mock her for taking such a drastic step. Ayesha also mentioned that their children had to drop out of school for some time since they did not have the money to pay their fees. But, once the business started growing, her husband witnessed people falling to their knees in gratitude at their doorsteps for the immeasurable good deeds they have done. He began to see the vision Ayesha was fighting for and became unwaveringly and extensively supportive of her endeavours. Ayesha's children, Abdullah and Soha Khan, are currently engaged in their studies but are involved in the business when they have the ability to and their help ranges from packing the meals to managing kitchen operations. In Fig. 7.1, you can see both the founders Sajid and Ayesha Khan along with some of the employees who work tirelessly in the kitchens. Around 50–60 people work in five kitchens in Ajman, Sharjah and Ras Al Khaimah (different cities in the UAE).

Food ATM has received numerous awards including securing a place in the Guinness World Records by delivering over 50,000 community meals in just 8 hours (see Fig. 7.2), leaving an indelible mark of compassion and achievement as well as the Authority of Social Contribution Award- Ma'an. This award was granted to those who have improved the lives of the needy educationally and socially. Food ATM also received an award from the Labour Standards Development Authority of Sharjah, as well as from the Weatherhead School of Management of Dubai University for helping to uplift and magnify SDG#2 of Zero Hunger.

Ayesha has helped to break the poverty cycle of marginalised communities in the UAE. The poverty cycle indicates how low income leads to low savings, which

Fig. 7.1.   The Founders of Food ATM Ayesha Khan and Sajid Along With Their Staff. *Source:* Ayesha Khan.

Fig. 7.2.   Guinness Book of Records Award. *Source:* Ayesha Khan.

leads to low investment, low productivity and the cycle is a continuous trap that affects three generations of a family (Cheng et al., 2016), which Ayesha and Food ATM has helped to shatter by providing them low-cost meals. Ayesha also sits on the Board of Directors of UN Global Compact – UAE Chapter and has been a vocal member of the UN High Level Political Forum in addressing major challenges faced by poor workers and their families.

SDG#1 No Poverty and Food ATM

The main target demographic of Food ATM are the blue-collar workers in the UAE. These labourers make a small salary, in which the bulk of the salary is sent back to the native countries of the labourers, and a meagre amount left supports the bare minimum of their survival here in the UAE. With Food ATM providing hot meals to labourers, their salary can be further utilised to give their families and themselves a better life. The result of Food ATM has allowed for generational poverty to end for some families, students [children of the labourers from India, Pakistan and Bangladesh] joyfully tell her about how they were able to accomplish their goals, secure medical degrees and attend school, consequently, elevating the living standards physically, emotionally, and mentally, therefore fulfilling SDG#1.1 which aims to eradicate extreme poverty for all people and SDG#1.2, which aims to reduce at least by half the proportion of men, women and children of all ages living in poverty (United Nations, 2023). Food ATM is also aligned with SDG#2 Zero Hunger. The elevation of living standards for the workers and their families is evident in the stories Ayesha has told of people falling to their knees in gratitude. Workers have told her that their families back home have been able to send their children to school, pay rent, move to a safer neighbourhood and have saved them from hunger and poverty. All this has been possible because Food ATM provides nutritious full meals at a cost of AED 3 to the needy workers or anybody who needs it, whereas the minimum cost of one meal in an inexpensive restaurant in the UAE is around AED 32 per person (Numbeo, 2024). These meals provided by Food ATM have reduced the workers expenses on food allowing them to be well fed and be productive at their hard labour bound work as well as to save money, thus allowing for more remittances to be sent back home and to better utilise their money in improving the family living conditions. SDG#1.5, which relates to building resilience in the poor and vulnerable to climate-related extreme events is fulfilled by Food ATM by reducing food costs and allowing the vulnerable to allocate their resources to improve their quality of life, houses, medical situations, thus making them less susceptible to these threats.

Food ATM also satisfies indicators SDG#1.a by partnering with various UAE government entities in order to diminish poverty. The social enterprise also engages with schools via student interaction with their waste management programs or through volunteering.

Food ATM also satisfies SDG#3 – Good Health and Well-being by serving food that includes fruits, whatever protein is available such as eggs, chicken, beef and ensuring that the food is good quality and hygienic. SDG#4 of good education is a direct result of the Food ATM, with the stress of food costs being alleviated by Food ATM, the children from poor communities have been able to receive a quality education due to money being saved because of the provided meals at a very economical rate. SDG#12 – Responsible Consumption and Production is an initiative that Food ATM has taken on and tackled. SDG#17, which involves an organisation facilitating various partnerships with several entities, has been satisfied by Food ATM as they have partnered with schools, UAE governmental agencies and even been recognised by universities such as Dubai University in terms of how positively impactful Food ATM has been.

Communicating SDG#1 With Internal and External Stakeholders

The idea of eliminating poverty was always the centre point of the business, every idea or initiative of the Food ATM business supports the idea of eliminating poverty. Ayesha spends most of her time in the kitchen supporting the team and ensuring efficient and quality work, while also making it a point to explain to the boys (the employees who make food in the kitchen, most of them come from a similar background and therefore they understand the purpose of this business very well and Ayesha considers them as her children) how important they are and how important the work they do is in improving the lives of other people, which she hopes acts as a point of motivation so the boys can put forth their best foot forward. Ayesha and her family feel blessed that the staff understands the severity of hunger and poverty and the importance of supporting a cause that aims to eliminate it. Whenever they are planning to open a new kitchen, Ayesha has regular meetings and inspires her boys; she tells them *Your presence there (new kitchen) will make the world's difference for the people there, so be the best.* This is a self-funded social enterprise therefore there are no direct stakeholders apart from Ayesha's direct family members. But she has been receiving an unimaginable amount of support from her suppliers, some of the government entities particularly the Ajman government. Ayesha believes the return on investment is the impact Food ATM has made on the society by supporting the poor and the hungry.

SDG#1 – Reporting and Measurement

Food ATM takes reporting and measurement quite seriously since Ayesha believes that *measuring the impact of Food ATM allows us for an understanding of the needs being met and the (nutrition) needs that need to be fulfilled. It is also for better allocation of resources and money.* Therefore, every 2 weeks or 10 days, they [Ayesha and Sajid] visit labour camps to know how things are changing for them. They document how cost inflation impacts life. They not only are focusing on reducing poverty and hunger in the UAE but are also concerned for the environment therefore are always looking to improve the process as well as solving some of the challenges to reduce their negative impact on the planet. In January 2024, they changed their packaging from plastic to biodegradable bags to pack the lunch. It is not only health and environmental conscious decision, but it keeps the food hot reducing the negative impact on the planet. This has led to reducing 40 kilograms of single use plastic bags going to the landfill daily.

Challenges and Opportunities of Working with SDG#1 No Poverty

Cost inflation is a huge challenge according to Ayesha. The more expensive food becomes, the more the poverty cycle is a continuous disaster in the lives of the needy and the more dependent people are on the Food ATM, which can be overwhelming. Additionally, at the start of Food ATM, Ayesha dealt with challenges of being a woman as men would underestimate and demean her, and she would have to take those insults head down since she had faith in the idea, and she quietly worked on it without worrying about what other people had to say. Today, she sits on the board of the UN Global Compact UAE Chapter as well as was recently invited to a meeting running up to High-Level Political Forum (HLPF) organised by Government Accelerators UAE and United Nations Global Compact UAE to discuss the challenges and to identify possible solutions. She highlighted that while remote locations in the UAE are undergoing significant development through various construction projects in desert areas, ensuring food security in these regions remains a challenge. The primary issue lies in the logistics of reaching these remote areas, which hampers the consistent and reliable distribution of food supplies. Despite the infrastructural advancements, the logistical barriers prevent effective food security measures from being implemented in all remote locations.

Another major challenge is a significant amount of food suitable for consumption is not utilised in a timely manner, resulting in large quantities being discarded into landfills. This inefficiency emphasises the critical need for improved food management and distribution practices to prevent waste and promote sustainability. Therefore, Food ATM has requested governments to support remote desert locations for 'food reach' using better transportation and storage facilities in the remote areas. Second, Food ATM has requested government authorities to establish a central reservoir in each Emirate to gather near-expiry food in terms of raw materials. These collected resources would be utilised to prepare daily meals, benefiting thousands of underprivileged individuals in the respective Emirates. Such initiatives will enhance the food security support system and reduce food waste. Ayesha also requested for an innovative initiative of combining Academia with Food Security & Agriculture to increase awareness about food loss and food production. Food ATM has provided hands-on experiences of farming to 7,000 students from 11 schools and 3 Universities in the UAE, wherein students do plantations and cook simple recipes on the farm, using organic products from the farm when they visit Food ATM facilities.

What Next for Food ATM and SDG#1

Ayesha believes that Food ATM should not be restricted to one entity or one location since food security and poverty is a global problem, and it needs urgent solutions. She hopes to see many more people from different countries come forward and take up this project in their location. She also mentioned that she intends to open at least one Food ATM centre per Emirate to bring relief to as many blue-collar workers as possible. They were not able to do it so far due to location challenges and lack of monetary support. Another very important dream Ayesha has is to further connect with schools around the UAE and create awareness about poverty, food loss and food security. Lastly, she says, *we'll do it until there is a day when there are no lesser privileged communities struggling to make ends meet.*

References

Cheng, T. L., Johnson, S. B., & Goodman, E. (2016). Breaking the intergenerational cycle of disadvantage: The three generation approach. *Paediatrics, 137*(6). https://doi.org/10.1542/peds.2015-2467

Global Media Insights. (2024, June 4). United Arab Emirates (UAE) population statistics 2024. *GMI Blog.* https://www.globalmediainsight.com/blog/uae-population-statistics/#:~:text=UAE%20Population%202024%20(Key%20Statistics,the%20research%20by%20GMI%20Team

National Committee on the Sustainable Development Goals. (n.d.). *The 2030 agenda for sustainable development United Arab Emirates.* National Committee on the Sustainable Development Goals. https://fcsc.gov.ae/en-us/Documents/SDG%20Report%20EN%20Final.pdf

Numbeo. (2024). *Cost of living in United Arab Emirates.* NUMBEO. https://www.numbeo.com/cost-of-living/country_result.jsp?country=United+Arab+Emirates

OECD. (2018). *The productivity-inclusiveness nexus.* OECD Publishing. https://doi.org/10.1787/9789264292932-en

United Nations. (2023). *Goal 1 | Department of economic and social affairs.* United Nations. https://sdgs.un.org/goals/goal1#targets_and_indicators

World Bank. (2020). *Productivity and innovation.* World Bank. https://www.worldbank.org/en/topic/competitiveness/brief/productivity-and-innovation

Index